ABERDEENSHIRE
LIBRARIES

WITHDRAWN
FROM LIBRARY

Aberdeenshire Library and Information Service
www.aberdeenshire.gov.uk/libraries
Renewals Hotline 01224 661511

HEADQUARTERS

20 DEC 2007
-5 MAR 2008
12 MAR 2008
HEADQUARTERS
13 OCT 2008
HEADQUARTERS
14 SEP 2009
-2 FEB 2019

HEADQUARTERS
-1 SEP 2014
-4 DEC 2014
23 MAR 2015
23 MAR 2015
-7 DEC 2019
17 MAR 2020

ABERDEENSHIRE
LIBRARIES
WITHDRAWN
FROM LIBRARY

ADAMSON, Eve

The golden
retriever

ALIS
2585576

THE GOLDEN RETRIEVER

Eve Adamson

Interpet Publishing

ABERDEENSHIRE LIBRARY AND INFORMATION SERVICES	
2585576	
HJ	570604
636.752	£12.99
AD	ANF

The Golden Retriever
An Interpet Book

Project Team
Editor: Heather Russell-Revesz
Copy Editor: Carl Schutt
Design: TR Lundquist and Angela Stanford
Series Design: Mada Design
Series Originator: Dominique De Vito

First published in UK by
Interpet Publishing
Vincent Lane
Dorking
Surrey
RH4 3YX

Copyright © 2007 by T.F.H. Publications, Inc.

All rights reserved. No part of this publication may be reproduced, stored, or transmitted in any form, or by any means electronic, mechanical or otherwise, without written permission from T.F.H. Publications, except where permitted by law. Requests for permission or further information should be directed to the above address.

ISBN13 978-1-84286-149-3

This book has been published with the intent to provide accurate and authoritative information in regard to the subject matter within. While every precaution has been taken in preparation of this book, the author and publisher expressly disclaim responsibility for any errors, omissions, or adverse effects arising from the use or application of the information contained herein. The techniques and suggestions are used at the reader's discretion and are not to be considered a substitute for veterinary care. If you suspect a medical problem consult your vet.

Interpet Publishing

TABLE OF CONTENTS

Chapter 1

HISTORY
of the Golden Retriever

Look into the dark brown eyes of a Golden Retriever and you'll see a friendly, enthusiastic, and trustworthy companion gazing back at you. You'll see a dog eager to be an active and loving family member, a best friend to adults, children, and other pets, a good listener, and a fellow adventurer in life. Whether your adventures take you up a mountain, down a river, across the country, around the block, or just far enough from the living room couch to grab a tasty snack from the kitchen, your Golden will be there at your side.

Most people recognise the Golden's feathery coat, floppy ears, and sociable ways, but may not be aware of how incredibly versatile, intelligent, and trainable this popular breed can be. The Golden Retriever can hunt and retrieve, enliven the household with his merry and affectionate presence, romp with the kids, or sit obediently waiting for the next instruction. Many Goldens compete in high-level obedience competitions, conformation shows, and field trials that test their natural retrieving ability. They sail over agility obstacle courses, revel in dock jumping competitions (the farthest jump into the water wins!), and wow audiences in the choreographed dance competition called canine freestyle. The sensitive Golden nose is well suited for organised tracking competitions to follow a scent, and many Goldens compete in a wide array of other canine sports, from catching a Frisbee to being part of a flyball relay race.

Golden Retrievers can earn Canine Good Citizen awards, which honour well-behaved and mannerly dogs, and many trainers agree that Goldens are among the easiest breeds to teach. Goldens have also distinguished themselves by being one of the best breeds for work as assistance dogs, leading the vision-impaired, helping the hearing-impaired, and assisting the mobility impaired. Some work at search and rescue, for law enforcement, as drug detection or bomb sniffing dogs, and as therapy dogs in nursing homes and hospitals.

Golden Retrievers even seem to have a supernatural sense about human health. Some Goldens have been trained to alert their owners to an impending seizure, even before the person knows the seizure is coming. Golden Retrievers

The Golden's delightful temperament, positive attitude, and easy trainability makes him among the best loved of any breed.

have even been trained to sniff out cancer cells with surprising accuracy. Goldens are truly versatile, active, and always ready for the next great game, fun activity, challenging job, or social occasion. For a Golden, life is a happy adventure, especially when a favourite human joins in the fun.

The Golden is among the best loved of any breed for his delightful temperament, positive attitude, easy trainability, and well-mannered behaviour, but for all this breed's fame and popularity, the Golden Retriever hasn't been around for very long. In fact, this breed has only been officially named the "Golden Retriever" for less than a century.

How did this handsome feather-coated retriever with his golden rainbow of shades evolve from a reliable Scottish hunting companion to one of the most popular breeds around today? Let's take a look back at the Golden's brief but exciting history.

GOLDEN BEGINNINGS

One of the first reasons why humans originally began to spend more time with dogs was because of the canine's innate ability to retrieve. Hunting becomes much easier with a dog who can sniff out and bring back the game—something a scent-challenged human can't do as easily or quickly as a dog. When hunting was the primary way that people could put food on the table, dogs with a particularly refined ability to retrieve, especially those with soft mouths (bringing back game intact by using their mouths carefully), served a crucial function. People began to breed dogs selectively, crossing the best hunting retrievers to help bring out their best qualities and minimise less desirable qualities.

In 19th century Europe, this selective breeding became somewhat of a competition. Which wealthy landowner could breed the best, fastest, most versatile, and most competent retriever? Each country's terrain, natural population of game animals, and hunting styles influenced which breeds evolved where, but few would disagree that in the British Isles many breeds evolved to become, essentially, the dogs we know today—spaniels, setters, pointers, scenthounds, terriers, collies, corgis, and of course, retrievers. When it comes to the sporting breeds—the spaniels, setters, pointers, and retrievers—the British gentry and the British peasantry each had their priorities, but both revolved around a single focus: helping humans bag the bird, whether on the wing, over the water, or in the bush.

All over England, Scotland, Ireland, and Wales, sporting breeds of all types evolved to meet the specific needs of different hunters, and before long, a segment of these dogs began to resemble the retrievers we know today. Some had short coats, like the Labrador Retriever or the Pointer. Some had long coats, like the Flat Coated Retriever or the Irish Setter. Some had curly coats, like the Curly Coated Retriever or the Irish Water Spaniel. Throughout most of history, none of these breeds were "official" or had consistent names from place to place—they were working dogs, hunting companions, and fellow travellers.

The problem for anyone wanting a precise history of any particular retriever breed lies in the mostly unrecorded breeding efforts of many of the landed gentry throughout the British Isles. While various members of the aristocracy might have had very specific ideas about how to refine or develop certain lines of retrievers (perhaps mixing in setters, water spaniels, pointers,

Puppy Coat

The Golden Retriever can trace his orgins back to Scotland. Much of Scotland is coastline, and developing a proficient and hearty water retriever was worth its weight in, well, gold.

Making a Golden Retriever

Breeds Likely Used to Create the Golden Retriever

- Wavy Coated (Flat-Coated) Retriever
- Tweed Water Spaniel (now extinct)
- Newfoundland
- Lesser St. John's Water Dog (ancestor to the Labrador Retriever)
- Irish Setter
- Bloodhound

or hounds to reinvigorate bloodlines and add desirable qualities such as different coat textures, scenting ability, or fondness for water), many of these breeding efforts will forever remain a mystery. Except for the efforts that produced the Golden Retriever!

Lucky for Golden Retriever fanciers and historians, the Golden Retriever's development is one golden exception. Thanks to the fastidious efforts of a Scottish Lord named Sir Dudley Marjoribanks (who later became Lord Tweedmouth), the Golden Retriever's history is an open book. Lord Tweedmouth purposefully shaped his breeding programme to "design" a dog that led to the Golden Retriever we know today. He kept careful records of all the dogs he crossed, when he crossed them, and who they produced. For these reasons, we know exactly how the Golden Retriever came to be.

When it comes to dog pedigrees, the records read somewhat like a family tree or a genealogical "X and Y then begat Z," but it is because of these records we can see exactly which breeds were used to create the Golden Retriever we know and love today. This not only answers questions of origin, but sheds light on some

Goldens were breed to have a great love of water retrieving.

of the Golden Retriever's characteristic traits, such as a love of water retrieving, dependable nature, eagerness to please, and that distinctive, feathery golden coat. Let's look at how it all happened.

Gold in the Highlands

While paintings have depicted yellow dogs that resemble the Golden Retriever throughout history, the Golden, as we know him today, began in Inverness-Shire, Scotland. Lord Tweedmouth desired a dog that could retrieve from both land and water, who could withstand the elements, and had the endurance to spend long days in the field. At the time, many people in Scotland hunted with retrievers called Wavy Coats. These retrievers probably evolved from a mix of different breeds, including local setters, spaniels, sheepdogs, and probably the Lesser St. John's Water Dog (the ancestor of the modern Labrador Retriever), and the Newfoundland (since Newfoundland was just across the North Atlantic, and trade with Britain was an active industry).

Another local breed, the Tweed Water Spaniel (now extinct), was known at the time for his reliable water retrieving, water-resistant coat, even temperament, and working ability. Many families depended on their Tweed Water Spaniels for their daily meals. Both the Wavy Coat and the Tweed Water Spaniel had qualities Lord Tweedmouth thought would contribute to create an even better retriever.

In 1864, Lord Tweedmouth bought a yellow puppy—the sole yellow pup in a litter of black wavy-coated retrievers—and named him Nous. The wavy-coated retrievers are the ancestors of today's flat-coated retrievers, and even today, these usually black dogs sometimes produce a yellow puppy. Lord Tweedmouth bred Nous with a Tweed Water Spaniel named Belle in 1868 and again in 1872. The first litter produced three female yellow puppies: Crocus, Cowslip, and Primrose; a female named Ada was born in the second litter. These four females became the foundation of Golden Retrievers as a distinct breed.

Cowslip proved to be a particularly pleasing specimen of a gold-coloured retriever. Lord Tweedmouth mated her with another Tweed Water Spaniel, and so the breeding efforts began. Historians believe a small Newfoundland (possibly for strength and heartiness), other Tweed Water Spaniels (for temperament and water retrieving skill), an Irish Setter (for colour, coat, and

Benched Shows

A benched show is a dog show where dogs wait in a separate "benching area" in an assigned spot, before and after their turn in the ring. Show attendees can visit the dogs and talk with the breeders and exhibitors in the benching area. Crufts dog show, the most famous dog show in the United Kingdom, is a benched show.

What is Line Breeding?

Back in 19th century Europe and Great Britain, line breeding (the practice of breeding dogs back to their relatives) wasn't very common, as it wasn't usually necessary and could sometimes result in compounding genetic problems. Line breeding is helpful, however, in trying to establish a breed that looks and acts the same from generation to generation—a breed that displays "type." In the case of the Golden Retriever, this practice helped to establish the unique Golden Retriever type (or look and quality), and contributed to the development of the Golden Retriever as a unique and individual breed.

bird-sense), and perhaps a Bloodhound (for high-level scenting ability) probably played important roles in the development of the Golden Retriever.

Later down the line, Cowslip was bred again, this time to a red Setter named Sampson. Their son, Jack, sired a second yellow retriever named Nous in 1884. The mother of this second Nous was named Zoe, and her parents were a black Wavy Coat Retriever and a female whose parents were Tweed and Cowslip.

Lord Tweedmouth's final studbook entry shows a mating between a dog named Queenie and the second Nous. The two yellow puppies resulting were named Prim and Rose, and these two dogs link all modern Golden Retrievers with Lord Tweedmouth's lines. Even though at the time the Golden was still

Retrievers were developed to meet the needs of different hunters.

considered a colour variation of the Wavy Coat Retriever, the Golden, as we know him today, was finally a unique breed.

Knowing that the first Goldens came from a cross between a large dog with a wavy golden coat and a medium-sized breed known for high intelligence, steady temperament, and a great love of water retrieving, proves that the Golden hasn't changed all that much from his original ancestry.

How Gold is Golden?

In the 19th and early 20th centuries, most Golden Retrievers were darker than the Goldens we know today. In the 1930s, people began to appreciate lighter-coloured Goldens, and the breed standards (the official written description of the ideal specimen of a particular dog breed) in both England and Scotland were changed to describe the proper Golden Retriever coat colour as allowing "any shade of gold or cream."

Today's breed standard simply describes the Golden Retriever's colour as "Any shade of gold or cream, neither red nor mahogany. A few white hairs on chest only, permissible." In the US the standard states "Rich, lustrous golden of various shades," but adds that extremely pale or extremely dark colours are undesirable.

THE GOLDEN COMES TO ENGLAND

With their love of dog shows and field trials, it didn't take long for retriever fanciers in England to hear about the new yellow variation of the familiar Wavy Coat Retriever. Soon the breed caught on in England, just as the sport of dog showing was becoming popular. At first, fanciers viewed this new yellow retriever as a variation of the Wavy Coat or Flat Coat Retriever, and grouped them all together. Many sportsmen used the dogs for retrieving in the field, and some competed in field trials with their new yellow retrievers, to test their retrieving abilities. The first Golden Retriever to win a field trial was in 1904, in England.

In 1904, the Kennel Club, England's national dog breed registry, recognised the first Golden Retrievers as a variation of the Wavy or Flat Coat Retrievers. This recognition allowed the breed to participate in dog shows. Four years later, the first "Flat-Coats (Golden)" were exhibited at England's Crystal Palace Dog Show, one of the most famous dog exhibition events in Europe. In 1913, the Kennel Club recognised the yellow/gold colour as a separate breed from the black Flat-Coats, and changed the name of the breed to Golden or Yellow Retriever. Soon, people began to drop the "Yellow" from the name, in favour of the more succinct term "Golden Retriever," and in 1920, the name "Golden Retriever" was finally recognised. The breed became more organised around this time when English fans of the breed started the first Golden Retriever Club.

One of the most influential English citizens to further the Golden Retriever was Lord Harcourt, whose Culham Kennels

Although originally developed for hunting, Goldens today are more likely to be beloved family pets.

produced many distinguished Golden Retrievers in the early 1900s, using two "foundation" dogs (the sire and dam or original parents of a kennel's breeding programme) named Culham Brass and Culham Rossa, both descendants of Lord Tweedmouth's Prim and Rose. A grandson of Brass and Rossa, named Ch. Noranby Campfire and owned by Mrs. Charlesworth from her Noranby Kennel, was the first Golden Retriever to finish his championship in a benched dog show in England, in 1913. The Noranby Kennel influenced Golden Retrievers in England through the 1950s, and the breed remains a favourite in England today, consistently ranking in the top ten most popular breeds.

THE GOLDEN COMES TO AMERICA

Americans knew about Golden Retrievers as early as the late 19th century. Lord Tweedmouth's son, the Honorable Archie Majoribanks, lived on a ranch in Texas with his Golden Retriever, Lady. Golden Retrievers came to America in greater numbers in the 1920s, when they could be exhibited in dog shows. In the 1920s,

Americans loved anything British, and this Anglophilic trend influenced the world of dog shows and the dog breeds Americans preferred.

The first Golden Retrievers were registered by the American Kennel Club in 1925, when Robert Appleton of Long Island registered his Golden Retrievers Lomberdale Blondin and Dan Hill Judy, which he had imported from England. At this time, Golden Retrievers were still exhibited together with all varieties of retrievers. In 1939, fanciers—mostly those based in Minnesota—formed the Golden Retriever Club of America, with John K. Wallace as president.

During the Second World War, Golden Retriever breeding stock became severely limited in Europe, and many breeders in England sent their dogs to the United States for safekeeping. However, throughout the early 20th century, even with this increased public awareness of the Golden Retriever, Goldens were still a rare breed in America! It was in the Midwest, however, that the Golden Retriever first thrived in the US. Many influential breeders and amazing dogs came out of this part of the country and helped to cement the Golden Retriever's reputation as an incomparable hunting companion and field trial winner.

When Colonel Samuel Magoffin of Vancouver, British Columbia, imported Speedwell Pluto from England in 1932, this gorgeous dog earned dog show championships in both Canada and the United States. Pluto was the first Golden Retriever ever to win a Best in Show at a dog show, and he also distinguished himself in the field. Colonel Magoffin founded kennels in both Vancouver and Colorado, and imported many dogs from England.

Colonel Magoffin's Midwestern relatives also became influential in breeding Golden Retrievers for show and field. The Midwest was the nation's centre for hunting upland game birds and waterfowl, so the Golden Retriever caught on quickly in America's heartland during the 1940s and 1950s. Col. Magoffin's brother-in-law, Ralph Boalt of Minnesota, imported many amazing Goldens from England, which produced some of the most influential field and show champions in America during this time. In fact, half the Golden Retriever litters registered with the American Kennel Club throughout the mid-1940s came from southeastern Minnesota.

The first Golden Retriever in America to compete in a field trial was Field Champion (FC) Rip, in 1939. Rip was from a litter of

Golden Guardians

Golden Retriever clubs are organisations comprised of people who love Goldens and want to be actively involved with them, either as breeders, dog show exhibitors, field trial competitors, obedience competitors, trainers, or pet owners. Some clubs are specialised, with members who shoot together, put on field trials, or rescue abandoned Golden Retrievers.

The Golden is one of the most popular dogs in the UK.

two English imports belonging to Mr. and Mrs. Mahlon Wallace Jr. and John K. Wallace of Saint Lewis. Rip remains one of the most accomplished field trial dogs, even today. The Wallaces took many British dogs from the influential Yelme Kennels into their own kennels during the war, and these dogs produced many field champions in America.

All About the KC and AKC

The Kennel Club (KC) is Britain's national all-breed club. They promote the sport of purebred dogs, hold dog shows (including the world's largest and most famous dog show, Cruft's), and educate the public about purebred dogs, dog training, dog health, responsible dog ownership, and much more.

The American Kennel Club (AKC), founded in 1884, is the most influential dog club in the United States. The AKC is a "club of clubs," meaning that its members are other kennel clubs, not individual people. The AKC registers purebred dogs, supervises dog shows, and is concerned with all dog-related matters, including public education and legislation. It collects and publishes the official standards for all of its recognised breeds. Their website offers many informative pages that relate directly or indirectly to Golden Retrievers.

At this time, most of the Golden Retrievers in America worked as gun dogs, but they slowly became more popular in the show ring because of their beautiful coats and outgoing personalities. For this reason, breeders worked to further beautify the Golden Retriever, but also to maintain and improve health, structure, and temperament, so the Golden Retriever would continue to be more and more valuable as a hunting companion.

The more people came to know the Golden Retriever, the more they were charmed not only by the Golden's happy personality, but by how easy

they are to train. The Golden has made its mark in Field Trials, in Working Trials and in Competitive Obedience. (This won't surprise anyone who has enjoyed the easy trainability of the Golden Retriever!)

Since those early days, Golden fanciers have never looked back. Today, the Golden Retriever has long enjoyed his spot as one of the most popular dogs in America. While many people still hunt with their Goldens, these merry dogs are much more likely to be beloved family members, assistance dogs, and personal companions; more likely to live in the house and sleep in the bedroom than out in a kennel; and more likely to be a confidant and friend rather than an "employee" valuable only during the shooting season.

The Golden deserves this spot of honour in the lives of humans. They listen to us, work for us, love to love us, and ask only that we love and care for them in return. And how could we refuse? Life is certainly sweeter when you've got a Golden.

Champion

Dogs earn the title of Champion, written "Ch." or "CH" at the beginning of their names, by winning or placing in enough dog shows to achieve the desired number of points.

Chapter 2 CHARACTERISTICS *of the Golden Retriever*

Friendly and active, gentle and easy to train—these characteristics describe a well-bred Golden Retriever, but they certainly don't tell the whole story. The Golden Retriever has many characteristics that make him such an accomplished athlete, proficient assistance dog, formidable obedience competitor, talented gun dog, and cherished family pet. Some of these qualities are physical—the size, weight, coat type, colour, head shape, tail set, and other attributes that make the Golden look the way he does. Some are more about the Golden's personality and inherent talents. It is the combination of all of these things that create the package we can instantly recognise and say: "There's a Golden Retriever! I love those dogs!"

A GOLDEN PICTURE

Ever since the Golden Retriever has been recognised as a unique breed, breeders have been working to make sure the Golden Retriever "breeds true"; that is, that Golden puppies look like their parents, and that all Golden Retrievers, at least to some degree, show "type."

How do breeders do this? They are, first and foremost, guided by the breed standard, an official written description of the ideal Golden Retriever. This breed standard, which is written by breed experts and approved by the Kennel Club in the UK and the American Kennel Club in the US, goes through each aspect of the Golden Retriever's shape, size, coat, and temperament, describing the ideal type.

Breeders use this standard to evaluate puppies in a litter to determine which most closely meet the standard and would be good prospects for future breeding efforts. Dog show judges also use this standard to evaluate dogs in the ring to

Golden Fact

The Golden Retriever comes from Scotland, and is one of England's most popular breeds.

determine which most closely resemble the picture described in the breed standard. While dog shows are a fun sport, their real purpose is to foster correct breed type in order to produce sound, healthy, beautiful Golden Retrievers who can fulfill their original purpose as a retrieving gun dog.

Of course, very few Golden Retrievers will look exactly like the ideal dog described in the breed standard. Your pet Golden Retriever needn't be exactly the right size or have exactly the right coat type (or head shape or ear set) for you to love him! But if you have a show dog and/or intend to breed your Golden Retriever, the breed standard becomes much more important. Even if you don't plan these activities for your Golden Retriever, you may be interested to learn what the ideal Golden Retriever is supposed to look like and how the ideal Golden Retriever is supposed to behave. It can also help you in choosing a breeder.

You won't find the KC and AKC breed standards verbatim in this chapter—instead, let's take a closer look at each part of the breed standard in more informal language. If you want to see the breed standards in their official form, you'll find them in the Appendix.

LET'S GET PHYSICAL

Breed standards get pretty technical about how a dog should

What Is a Breed Standard?

Every purebred dog has a unique look, and if breeders didn't breed to preserve that look, we would lose many of the beloved and cherished purebred dogs we know today. Can you imagine the world without Golden Retrievers, Chihuahuas, Great Danes, or German Shepherds?

Luckily, purebred dog enthusiasts write breed standards to describe what each purebred dog should look like. Breed standards typically describe a breed's overall appearance, then go into detail about size, coat type, colour, head shape, body shape, leg shape, tail set, ear set, eye shape, and many other details. Breed standards also often describe a breed's expected or ideal temperament.

In the United Kingdom, national "parent" breed clubs for each recognised breed receive recognition from the Kennel Club, submit their breed standards for review and approval, then publish these breed standards to help breeders in their breeding programmes and dog show judges in their evaluations of show dogs. You can find the written breed standards for all the breeds the Kennel Club recognises on the KC web site.

The Fédération Cynologique Internationale (FCI) is the world canine organisation that promotes purebred dogs. At FCI shows, judges use the 'country of origin' standard for each breed that is exhibited.

For a Golden Retriever, the breed standard describes a dog that will be best at doing his job as a hunting retriever.

look, but there is a reason behind the detail. For Golden Retrievers, the breed standard is meant to describe the physical dog that will be best at doing his job—in this case, working as a hunting retriever. For that reason, Goldens need to be strong, athletic, and resilient. They should have a weatherproof coat and proper structure that won't break down under heavy physical activity. They also need the patience to wait in a duck blind for hours, the heartiness and energy to retrieve through undergrowth or cold water, the strength to last all day in the field, and the temperament that urges them to look to their humans for direction rather than getting their own ideas about how things should go. (Some breeds such as hounds who have to travel far distances from their humans need to make hunting and tracking decisions on their own.)

There is another side to the Golden Retriever's physical self, however. Simply, people who love the way Golden Retrievers look and who find them beautiful want very much to preserve that beauty. So, the breed standard also describes certain aspects that make a Golden Retriever look like a Golden Retriever, whether or not those features directly affect working ability. For example, a dense and water-repellent coat is important for the Golden's working ability, but does it really matter if that coat colour is extremely pale or extremely dark? Not for hunting ability, but it does matter if you want your Golden Retriever to have the breed characteristic of a golden colour.

General Appearance

The first section of the breed standard describes the Golden Retriever's general appearance and calls for a powerful and active dog that is balanced and well put together. That means that no one part of the Golden Retriever should take precedence over the Golden Retriever as a whole picture. Does the dog look like a Golden Retriever? Does he look like all his parts match? If a Golden's head is too big, legs too long, coat too bushy, or tail swings up behind him like a Husky, that doesn't say "Golden Retriever."

Goldens should also be built to work—they should look muscular and in good shape. When they move, it should be efficient and coordinated, not wobbly, stumbling, or crooked. A good Golden should look like he could retrieve ducks or pheasants from sunrise to sunset without tiring or losing enthusiasm.

Show Versus Field Goldens

All good breeders want their dogs to be healthy, but as breeders breed for both working ability and looks, different lines can start to diverge in different ways, depending on the individual sub-priorities of breeders. Many breeds eventually begin to split into working types and show types, and the Golden Retriever is no exception. Go to a dog show, and the Golden Retrievers you see will look similar to, but also markedly different than the Golden Retrievers you will see at a high-powered field trial event.

Field trial breeders breed for strength, stamina, and drive. These leaner, smaller Goldens tend to have less coat (which can get tangled in undergrowth or matted after frequent dips in the water). They also tend to have more active, high-energy, go-go-go temperaments. Show Goldens tend to be bigger, heavier in bone, with more coat (because lots of beautiful silky Golden fur is aesthetically pleasing). They may not look as lean and athletic as field Goldens because they spend more time on the road doing the show circuit than in the field.

This difference greatly concerns many breeders and fanciers who believe that Goldens should be both beautiful and fully capable of hunting with great stamina and strength. Some people try to show Goldens and also compete with them in field trials, but this is relatively uncommon. More common are show dogs that also work as "weekend hunters" with their owners, and field trial dogs who also enjoy a place as an active family pet. Other retrievers, notably Labrador Retrievers, also have experienced this "show vs. field" split. Be sure to inquire whether the breeder you are visiting breeds for show or field, as this can influence the temperament and energy level of your pet.

The Golden Retriever's expressive face is one of his most defining characteristics.

Size Matters

The Golden Retriever is a medium-sized dog. Not small like a terrier, but certainly no Saint Bernard or Great Dane, either. According to the breed standards, Golden Retrievers should be about the same size as most other retrievers, like Labrador Retrievers and Chesapeake Bay Retrievers, although each breed's standard has very specific height specifications that all differ slightly from each other, some allowing for a greater range of heights than others.

The Golden Retriever, according to the standard, should measure about 22 to 24 inches from the ground to the top of the shoulder for males, and 20 to 22 inches for females. You will sometimes see pet Golden Retrievers that are taller or shorter than this standard, but for show dogs, more than one inch above or below the standard will be faulted in the show ring. This encourages breeders to keep breeding Golden Retrievers to a standard size that is—in the opinion of the original writers of the standard—most suited to the Golden Retriever's job as an able-

Why so much emphasis on teeth? A retriever retrieves with his mouth, of course! Golden Retrievers must have healthy, sound mouths that can easily pick up and gently retrieve game without mauling it and without constantly dropping it.

bodied working retriever.

The KC standard does not stipulate weight, but generally male Golden Retrievers should weigh between 65 and 75 pounds, females between 55 and 65 pounds. Again, pet Goldens may vary from this standard, especially when they become overweight! Goldens should get their weight from good, sturdy bones and well-developed muscles, not from fat.

The breed standard also addresses Golden Retriever's proportions. Golden Retrievers shouldn't be quite square (a term to describe a dog that is about the same height from shoulder to ground as he is from the front of the breastbone to the back of the buttocks), but almost. Golden Retrievers should be just slightly longer than tall, at a ratio of 12:11. (How's that for specific?)

Heads Up

The Golden Retriever's head is an important part of what makes a Golden Retriever look like a Golden Retriever. The head encompasses the characteristics of the skull shape, muzzle, eyes, ears, nose, teeth, and expression, the latter being one of the most defining characteristics of the Golden Retriever. Remember that even more important than head is an overall balance and sense of "type," but admittedly, quite a lot of the sense of "type" in a Golden Retriever comes from the head.

The Golden Retriever should have a broad skull and a straight muzzle that blends smoothly into the skull. The Golden's head shouldn't look delicate like a Greyhound or flat-faced and round like a Bulldog, either. It is the quintessential "typical dog" shape of head, with the muzzle approximately as long as the skull and a defined but not overly exaggerated stop (the angle at which the muzzle meets the skull).

Mouth and Teeth

From the side, the Golden Retriever's muzzle should be just slightly broader at the stop than at the tip, not tapering into a pointy muzzle but remaining strong with plenty of room for a good nose and mouth with all the teeth in the right alignment. That alignment should be a scissor bite, where the top teeth close just over the front of the bottom teeth in a nice neat closure. If the teeth meet edge-to-edge in a level bite, a show dog would be faulted for this. However, an undershot bite (an underbite where the top teeth close behind the bottom teeth, like a Bulldog) or an overshot bite (where the top teeth close well in front of the bottom teeth with a space between them) is even worse.

Eyes

The Golden Retriever's eyes should be dark and relatively large (a beady-eyed Golden wouldn't look characteristic), but not protruding like a Pug's. The dark brown colour emphasises the Golden's friendly, warm-hearted expression, and the Golden's eyes should reflect his temperament. They should also have nice, tight lids that don't gape or roll in or out or show any haw (the red membrane inside the lower eyelid, exposed in some breeds such as Bloodhounds). The Golden's eyes are very important in expressing type and should be full of joyful enthusiasm and open-hearted responsiveness.

Ears

The Golden Retriever's ears also affect the overall expression. They should be short and neatly floppy, well above and behind the eyes. If you take the tip of your Golden's ear and pull it over the eye, it should just cover one eye. Goldens don't have low, long hound-dog ears or short, pointy terrier ears. When your Golden perks up, his ears may also perk up, but they should never stand erect or fall to the sides. They are moderate in all ways, and when held naturally, the tips should fall close to the cheek.

Nose

The Golden's nose should be dark like his eyes. Lighter, pale noses detract from the Golden's look, although some Goldens do have noses that get lighter in cold weather (called a winter nose), a perfectly natural condition. For show dogs, the darker the nose and eyes, the better, although many perfectly lovely Golden Retrievers have medium-brown eyes and noses.

Neck and Body

The Golden Retriever has a strong, muscular, long (but not too long) neck that should flow gracefully into the shoulders. Too much neck will detract from the Golden's look of strength, but the Golden shouldn't be short-necked, either, as that would make him look stumpy. From the side, the line from the base of the neck to the base of the tail (called the topline) should be straight, with just a gentle slight slope at the croup, or the area just before the base of the tail. Show dogs will be faulted for a totally flat or too-sloped croup, as well as for a back that caves in (called a swayback) or curves upward (called a roachback).

The Golden Retriever's body is just slightly longer from the breastbone to the rump as it is tall, from the top of the shoulders (the withers) to the ground, and the Golden's chest should be deep enough, with ribs broad enough, to hold large lungs that will help the Golden swim well and have greater endurance. That doesn't mean the Golden should be barrel chested, however. The body should look balanced, and all the parts should fit together. The chest should extend down to the Golden's elbow, and the Golden should have plenty of chest space between the two front legs.

Tail

That beautiful feathered tail should flow directly out from the back and be thick and muscular at the base. When held down, the bone of the tail shouldn't reach below the Golden's hock (the ankle joint, which in dogs is typically well above the ground and easy to mistake for a knee unless you notice which way the joint bends). The proper Golden Retriever tail extends straight out or will curve slightly upward, especially when the Golden is excited. It shouldn't curl up over the back, however. The tail should be feathered along the underside.

From the Front

If you look at your Golden Retriever straight on, you should see strong, muscular front legs and shoulder blades set nicely back and close together, allowing for freer, easier movement. Legs should be straight and strong with a moderately heavy bone that suggests strength and athleticism. The part of the Golden's leg between the wrist (carpus) and the foot is the pastern, and it should be short and strong, not wobbly or too dramatically angled. The Golden's feet should be medium-sized and nicely compact, round, with thick pads and strong knuckles, allowing the Golden to be on his feet retrieving for hours without suffering from weak feet or worn pads. The Golden's toes shouldn't be splayed apart, although this can happen if you allow the nails to get too long. Some Goldens have a lot of hair between the paw pads, and trimming this hair will show

Paw Pads

Trimming the hair between the paw pads can prevent debris from collecting there.

The Golden Retriever's strongly muscled hindquarters contribute to his strong, efficient movement.

off the Golden's foot as well as prevent dirt, ice, and other debris from getting caught between the paw pads.

From the Back

Your Golden's rear view should reveal broad, strongly muscled hindquarters with a hip joint bent at about a 90 degree angle, which contributes to strong, efficient movement. The Golden's knees (stifles) should also be angled enough for good movement and the hocks or ankle joints strong and straight. As in the front, the pasterns should also be short and strong, and the feet in the back should match the feet in the front. From behind, the Golden's legs should be straight, not bent in with knees pointing toward each other (cow-hocked) or out to the side (spread-hocked) at the knee.

Coat and Colour

One of the Golden Retriever's most obvious characteristics is his beautiful, silky, feathery golden coat. The coat should repel water and keep the Golden protected from the elements, and its colour should be a rich, lustrous gold. The KC standard specifies only that the colour should be any shade of gold or cream, but red or mahogany is not permissible. The AKC standard asks for a rich, lustrous gold, and faults extremely pale or dark coats.

Movement

Golden Retrievers should trot with a free and easy gait that shows power and endurance as well as coordination, allowing the Golden to move efficiently for long periods without tiring. Well-bred Golden Retrievers will be built in a way to best maximise powerful, efficient movement.

Temperament

The breed standard describes the Golden's temperament as "kindly, friendly and confident." Correct Golden temperament should not be shy or nervous, nor aggressive or hostile. Temperament is more than just a side note for the Golden Retriever. It is one of the most important traits, and without the characteristic friendly, reliable, warm temperament, a Golden Retriever simply isn't a Golden Retriever. Temperament

Fédération Cynologique Internationale

While many people have only heard of the American Kennel Club, Kennel Club, and perhaps some other national kennel clubs, an international organisation actually exists. The Fédération Cynologique Internationale is the World Canine Organization, which includes 80 members and contract partners (one member per country), each of which issues its own pedigrees and trains its own judges. The founding nations were Germany, Austria, Belgium, France, and the Netherlands. It was first formed in 1911 but later disappeared during World War I. The organisation was reconstituted in 1921. Currently, neither the United States nor Canada is a member.

The FCI ensures that its pedigrees and judges are recognised by all FCI members. Every member country conducts international shows as well as working trials; results are sent to the FCI office, where they are input into computers. When a dog has been awarded a certain number of awards, he can receive the title of International Beauty or Working Champion. These titles are confirmed by the FCI.

The FCI recognises 331 dog breeds, and each of them is the "property" of a specific country, ideally the one in which the breed developed. The owner countries of the breeds write the standard of these breeds in cooperation with the Standards and Scientific Commissions of the FCI, and the translation and updating are carried out by the FCI.

In addition, via the national canine organisation and the FCI, every breeder can ask for international protection of his or her kennel name.

comes both from good breeding and good management, but good breeding provides the foundation for that classic Golden temperament that gives trainers, handlers, and pet owners something wonderful to build upon.

WHAT ARE GOLDENS REALLY LIKE?

Golden Retrievers have a reputation as the perfect family dog, and their reputation is well earned…sort of. People dream of a friendly, mellow dog to keep them company, play with their kids, go walking or shooting, and generally hang around the house being helpful and charming. That description fits many well-trained adult Golden Retrievers, but what many people don't realise is that Golden Retrievers don't come preprogrammed for perfection.

Because they have been bred over the centuries to do a job that requires a lot of energy and endurance, Golden Retrievers have just that…a lot of energy and endurance! Especially when they are puppies and adolescents, Golden Retrievers need a lot of exercise

The Golden Retriever's happy nature and friendly ways make him a joy to have in the family.

or they will probably channel that energy less productively, such as with destructive chewing, jumping on people (in adolescence, a large Golden Retriever can easily knock down a small adult), digging large holes in the garden, or barking more than is necessary.

Fortunately, the Golden's heritage also gives him some of his most endearing qualities. Good hunting dogs must take to training quickly and with enthusiasm, so housetraining and basic commands come easily to the Golden Retriever. But they don't come pretrained, so pet owners must do some work to get their Goldens to that place where they can earn the title of "perfect family dog." Because Goldens are quick to learn and sensitive, they don't need harsh training methods. They need only consistency, a fun approach to training, and lots of positive reinforcement for a job well done.

The Golden Retriever's happy nature and friendly ways make him a joy to have in the house. He is good at cheering up his people when they are having a bad day, romping with the kids, and getting excited about each and every walk around the block. Goldens aren't typically picky eaters, shy, nervous, or even excessively barky. A well-bred Golden is even tempered and a good judge of character.

Untrained and unsocialised Golden Retrievers are another matter. Like any breed, Goldens who aren't taught good manners and exposed to friendly people and dogs early in life can be pushy, nippy, aggressive, hyperactive, and destructive. Regular training and lots of positive, safe life experience is the way to bring out the very best in your Golden Retriever, so that his true nature and personality can shine.

IS A GOLDEN FOR YOU?

Golden Retrievers may be popular, but many of them are also abandoned to rescue centers when people who aren't suited for this breed adopt them and then give up on them. Many people, families, and living environments work well with Golden Retrievers, but this breed isn't for everyone. Pet ownership is a commitment. That means a good pet owner is prepared to put time, money, and energy into proper veterinary care, training, quality food, supplies, and invest quality time into building the relationship between human and dog.

It's easy to romanticise pet ownership before you bring home that frisky puppy, but the reality of living with a dog isn't always fun. Puppies require housetraining. They chew things you don't

Golden Retrievers can learn to live happily with cats, as long as they are introduced carefully.

want them to chew. They require vaccinations, worming, and check-ups. They need obedience training and socialisation, too.

Adolescence is no easier! Adolescent Goldens are big, boisterous, and haven't yet grown into their gangly bodies. Their energy levels are akin to human teenagers, and they can get themselves into trouble. This stage, which can occur anywhere between 8 and 12 months (and can sometimes last beyond the first year), is the stage when Golden Retrievers most often end up in rescue centres. If you can ride out adolescence, you'll enjoy many happy and calm years with your Golden, so it pays to be prepared to deal with this challenging stage.

In old age, Goldens may suffer from many different diseases and disorders associated with ageing, from joint problems like arthritis and hip dysplasia to eye diseases, cancer, heart problems, and many other conditions similar to those ageing humans experience. Veteran Goldens need more frequent check-ups, tests, and vet care than Goldens in their prime, and the committed pet owner will provide this care, along with sensitivity towards an ageing Golden's changing needs.

Here's how to determine whether a Golden Retriever is the breed for you.

Your Living Environment

The first thing to consider before bringing home a Golden Retriever is your living environment. Goldens are adaptable dogs and can thrive in many different living spaces, from an urban apartment to rural acreage. That doesn't mean every house, garden, and area is right for a Golden, however. Do you have a home full of precious, breakable objects that you want to keep on display, and will you get upset if an enthusiastically wagging Golden's tail clears off that shelf of knick-knacks in a single wag? Do you object to pet hair? Do you have a large garden with a fence? All of these and other characteristics of your living environment can influence your experience of owning a Golden Retriever, so consult this list before you decide:

- ***Do you have a fenced garden?*** Golden Retrievers like to spend time outside, and they need room to run, but can't be trusted not to run away, especially when they are young and haven't yet learned the rules. A large fenced garden is ideal for a Golden Retriever, but they can also live in apartments or small gardens as long as they get plenty of exercise with you in the form of long walks, trips to the park, or active play in a safely enclosed area.
- ***Do you have other pets?*** Golden puppies can easily learn to live happily with other dogs and even cats, but Golden Retrievers

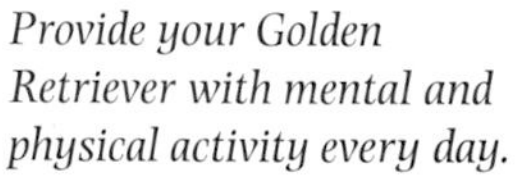

Provide your Golden Retriever with mental and physical activity every day.

Children and Dogs

Children love dogs, and dogs love kids. Here's how to make the most of a great combination:

- Socialise young dogs by safely and positively exposing them to many different children, so they understand that children are just smaller, livelier, more enthusiastic versions of adults—with a higher play drive!
- Socialise young children to dogs by supervising at all times and teaching children the polite and gentle way to handle a dog. That means no ear tweaking, tail yanking, eye poking, fur pulling, or riding the dog.
- Provide kids and dogs with lots of organised activities to do together. Initiate a game of fetch, Frisbee, or tag, and sit back to watch the fun. This lays the groundwork for teaching kids how to work with dogs.
- Take your older kids to puppy classes and basic obedience classes. They will learn a lot about managing your dog, and the time together will help build the relationship between the dog and the child.
- If your child shows interest, let him or her continue on with training classes.
- Let your child spend some time every day training the dog and offering treats. Keep training sessions light, short, and fun. This regular interaction is great for both the dog and the child.
- Always supervise, supervise, supervise.
- Admire the blossoming relationship between your kids and your dogs!

are likely to chase cats they don't know, not to mention stray hamsters or loose parakeets. While Goldens typically get along well with other dogs, introduce new pets carefully and gradually to be sure everyone feels comfortable and gets along. Golden Retrievers may not tend to be dog aggressive, but some Goldens just don't get along with certain dogs, in the same way certain people don't get along. Call it chemistry, but it happens (even though with Goldens, it is rarer than with many other breeds). Goldens that have not been castrated or spayed may be more likely to object to same-sex dogs, but in most cases, Goldens are generally happy to have another animal to play with.

- ***Do you love to vacuum?*** Golden Retrievers shed all year, picking up the pace of shedding in the spring and the autumn. That means a lot of vacuuming, and tolerance for the occasional (or more than occasional) stray Golden hair on your pillow, rug, and even in your morning coffee.
- ***Do you have dog-friendly décor?*** Goldens also like to bound around the house, play actively, and their long swishy tails may knock over breakables. Super-fastidious housekeepers need not apply. (Unless you like the challenge of designing for maximum efficiency in the presence of a big yellow dog! You wouldn't be

Keeping Active

A young Golden Retriever needs at least an hour or two of physcial activty every day.

the first to install blonde carpeting and develop a minimalist approach to decorating just for the sake of your dog.)

- ***Are you sure you want a dog around...all the time?*** Goldens won't be happy if left confined to a small dog run or a utility room most of the time. Goldens want to be where the action is, where the people are...with you. They want to sleep on your bed, follow you into the bathroom, play with you in the swimming pool, and sit with you on the couch. The best environment for a Golden is at your side, with free run of the house (after housetraining, of course), so he can feel like a part of the family and the home.
- ***How do you feel about your furniture?*** Do you really need to keep your Golden off the bed? Or maybe just off the new sofa, but the old love seat is fine? Your Golden will bargain with you for comfort privileges, and Goldens enjoy at least a little bit of furniture lounging—preferably with you beside them. (If you can't resist letting your Golden on the bed, don't worry. You are in the majority!)

Move It or Lose It

Are you active? Especially with young Golden Retrievers, whose energy seems to know no bounds, pet owners must be prepared to provide plenty of exercise, and that doesn't mean letting your Golden out in the garden and leaving him there. Golden Retrievers want to be active with you, so long walks or runs, bike rides, hikes, hunting excursions, or active games of retrieving are necessary to keep your Golden well exercised and out of trouble. If you are used to getting your exercise at the gym, you may want to rethink your fitness endeavours to include your Golden. Luckily, exercise is good for both of you!

Many people have the image of a Golden with a calm, mellow personality, but this is typical of older dogs; it isn't fair to expect this kind of tranquil self-possession of a puppy or adolescent Golden Retriever. The key to living happily with a young Golden is to provide a high level of mental and physical activity for at least an hour or two each day (your Golden could easily do more). Then, your puppy or young adult dog will be happy to collapse for a well-deserved nap.

Don't worry, your Golden will slow down quite a bit as he ages. That doesn't mean he (or you) should quit exercising, but just like with people, adults don't typically have that overflowing energy of young kids or adolescents. Give your Golden a few years of good exercise and training, and before you know it, he will resemble those mellow, laid-back Golden Retrievers you have so often admired.

Kids and Goldens: Potential Siblings?

Goldens are friendly creatures, and that means the more people around to play with, the better. Kids, in particular, make a perfect match for Goldens. Who better to throw that ball over and over again? Kids love to play games, teach tricks, and even brush the Golden's pretty coat. Goldens love the energy, spirit, and joy children exude. A match made in heaven?

Maybe. Living with Goldens and children requires planning and some firm rules. If you bring a Golden puppy into your home, you must teach your children the correct, gentle way to handle the puppy. Puppies are not stuffed animals and shouldn't be poked, prodded, ridden, or roughly handled. Tails and ears are not for pulling! Likewise, Goldens must be trained to play gently with children. Many older Goldens sense how boisterous they can be with a child, but younger Goldens tend to get overly enthusiastic and could accidentally knock over a small child.

Most importantly, never leave any child alone with any dog for any length of time unsupervised. You never know what could happen when you aren't watching. Better safe than sorry, and supervision is safest for both kids and dogs.

That being said, many a Golden Retriever has sat patiently at the side of a child who pours out his heart to his best friend. Goldens can retrieve for as long as a child wants to throw a ball or a Frisbee. They love to run, jump, play, swim—all the things kids love. They also like serving as a pillow during TV time and are convenient dispatchers of those bits of dinner kids would really rather not eat. When well socialised and trained, Golden Retrievers might just be the best possible breed for children and families.

Chapter 3

PREPARING for Your Golden Retriever

You have your mind made up. A Golden Retriever is the breed for you. Now what? Bringing home a Golden Retriever and making him a part of your life may sound easy, but it pays to make a couple of informed decisions first. Do you really want a puppy, or might an adult Golden be better for your particular situation? How do you go about finding a reputable breeder that specialises in producing typical Golden Retrievers? And what about the rescue centre, or a Golden Retriever rescue group? Would one of these be the best place to find the Golden of your dreams?

This chapter will help you to explore your options. After that, find out how to prepare your home for your new Golden Retriever: how to puppy-proof your house, what supplies you will need, how to make sure your Golden Retriever has reliable identification, and what to do with your Golden Retriever once you get him home. What happens when you have to go to work? Or on holiday? Or when you just don't feel like going on a walk? We'll explore those concerns, too.

Knowing exactly what you want and making the effort to find the right dog for you will certainly pay off later, giving you and your Golden the best possible start to a happy life together. Most importantly, even though you may be impatient to get that Golden home, try not to be in a rush. Take your time finding the perfect dog, rather than being seduced by the first lovable, fuzzy yellow mug you meet. Too many Goldens are abandoned to rescue groups each year due to rash decisions and impulse buys made by uninformed pet owners. Better to get prepared and find the Golden you know you can stick with for the rest of his life. You'll both be glad you did your homework.

BIG GOLDEN, LITTLE GOLDEN?

Who could possibly resist a Golden Retriever puppy? That silky fur, those big brown eyes, so cute and rambunctious and just the right size for cuddling! But wait one minute. Sure, Golden Retriever puppies are cute, but they also take a lot of work. Even though they are easier to housetrain than some breeds, you'll still need to take the time to housetrain them. They have to learn how to behave in the house, and in the yard, and on walks. And oh, how those puppies need to chew, chew, chew! Puppies need a lot of supervision, training, socialisation, and work during their first year. They also need frequent vet visits for vaccinations, and those first months of a puppy's life are key for developing a solid temperament, self-confidence, and good manners. Are you sure you are up to that kind of a job?

Some people will answer with an enthusiastic "yes!" and if that's you, great. Raising a Golden Retriever puppy is a demanding but highly rewarding task. You get to enjoy those puppy antics, you get to take lots of "baby" pictures, you get to watch your Golden Retriever explore and learn about the world, and that can be a lot of fun. You get to train your puppy from the very beginning, assuring that he learns the rules in your house and bonds with you right away. When your Golden Retriever matures, you get to remember those puppy months with fondness. You'll have puppy stories to share, and if you are like some zealous Golden owners, you'll have a few photo albums and some digital movie footage to show your friends. ("Now *this* one is when Buster was five months old, right after he chewed that hole in the seat of my pyjamas, and no, I wasn't wearing them at the time! Oh, and here's the one where he gutted the recliner cushions...good times, good times!")

Raising a Golden Retriever puppy is a demanding but highly rewarding task.

Before you start looking, decide if a puppy or adult Golden is right for you.

On the other hand, if you aren't crazy about that whole puppy thing, an adult Golden Retriever may be perfect for you. Many adult Goldens need homes and are already well-trained, responsible canine members of society, fully housetrained, well past the teething stage, and relatively calm. Goldens are an adaptable breed, and while many will mourn the loss of a previous owner, they also quickly adjust to anyone who gives them good food, a comfortable place to live, and plenty of loving attention. You can still bond with your Golden, even if you didn't raise him from puppyhood. In fact, many Golden owners say that adult Goldens they adopted from rescue centres seem so grateful to be with a loving owner that they bond to their people with particular intensity.

Adult Goldens may be retired show dogs, family pets whose owners weren't able to keep them anymore for any number of reasons, or strays picked up from the streets whose histories no human can know. Whatever the case, if you decide to adopt an adult Golden Retriever, you can feel good about giving a home to a Golden who needs one. The only downside to adopting an adult Golden Retriever is that you won't have as long a time to spend together. And of course, you won't have all those puppy pictures (but maybe you can make do with a *Golden Puppies* calendar instead).

MALE OR FEMALE?

Golden Retriever breeders report that most people seeking a Golden Retriever as a pet think they want a female. And why not? Female Golden Retrievers don't get as big as males and tend to be slightly less rambunctious, especially as adolescents. However, in reality, the individual personality of the Golden Retriever makes more of a difference than the gender. Some Goldens are extremely energetic and driven, while others tend to be more laid back, regardless of gender. Talk to your breeder about what kind of personality you would prefer in a Golden, rather than what gender you think you want.

Some people also believe that females tend to be a little more independent, strong willed, and stubborn, while males tend to be more affectionate and even needy. Females often make excellent hunting companions and field trial competitors, while males make excellent pets for active families who like to take their dogs wherever they go. Again, individual personality is more important than gender, so trust the breeder to help you choose the best puppy, rather than the best gender.

WHERE TO FIND THE DOG OF YOUR DREAMS

Since the Golden Retriever is such a popular breed, finding one for sale is not difficult. And maybe that puppy you see advertised is a good Golden Retriever for you, but that doesn't mean you should rush out right now with your chequebook in hand. First, consider all your options. You can find Golden Retrievers at a breeder or

Health Matters

Today, breeders are increasingly accountable for the health of the dogs they show and breed, and you can look up Golden Retriever puppies in an online open database to ensure the breeder has done health tests on the parents of a litter, and sometimes on the puppies themselves. Health tests are very important for several reasons. All breeds, including Golden Retrievers, are prone to certain genetic diseases. Qualified veterinary practitioners can detect many of these diseases early, either by DNA tests or by physical examinations. Breeders who have these tests performed on their dogs know which dogs to breed and which dogs to remove from a breeding programme, so they don't continue to perpetuate genetic disease. All of this work (and expense!) is in the service of eliminating unhealthy Golden Retrievers from the gene pool while preserving the breed's best qualities: working ability, beauty, and that friendly and agreeable Golden Retriever temperament. Buying a Golden Retriever from an ethical breeder decreases your chances of having a Golden who will develop a health problem later in life. Of course, any dog can get a disease or disorder, especially as they age. But why not give your Golden the best possible chance of good health and a long life?

Good breeders make sure their Goldens have just the right temperament to make an excellent family pet.

at a local rescue centre. Each has its positives and negatives. Take time to decide which route to choose. Let's take a closer look at the options available.

Breeders

Buying a Golden Retriever from a breeder may sound complicated, but this is actually an excellent way to purchase a Golden Retriever puppy. The trick is to find a knowledgeable, experienced, responsible show dog breeder. Why would you want a breeder breeding dogs for the show ring when you just want a pet? Because show breeders have several very important priorities in breeding Golden Retrievers. Rather than breeding for the profit they can reap from selling puppies, show breeders are devoted to bettering the Golden Retriever as a breed. To win in a show ring, a Golden Retriever must be well built, must look like a Golden Retriever is supposed to look (according to the breed standard), and must be healthy.

Good breeders do more than breed for good health and beauty.

Show or Field?

If you plan to hunt with your Golden Retriever, or like the idea of participating in dog sports, field trials, or other high-intensity physical activities, you might also consider finding a breeder who specialises in field dogs. These Golden Retrievers are not bred to the breed standard for show dogs. Instead, they are bred for high drive, intensity, athleticism, and working ability. They may be somewhat smaller, rangier, and have a less dense and fluffy coat. These dogs are bred to be serious athletes. Generally, field dogs may be too active and intense for a typical pet home, but highly active people may prefer them, so think about what kind of pet you want and what kind of activities you plan to do with your Golden. Do you want a Golden with some serious get-up-and-go, or do you prefer a mellower buddy to hang around the house with you?

They also breed for good temperament. Breeders know that in any given litter of puppies, only one or two will be show prospects. The other puppies may not have quite the right ear set, eye shape, size, or coat quality to be a serious contender in the show ring, and guess what happens to those puppies? They go to pet homes. But not just any pet homes! Good breeders have devoted their lives to Golden Retrievers and aren't going to sell their precious Golden babies to just anybody. You may find yourself being grilled by the breeder: Do you have a fenced garden? How much time do you have to spend with your Golden? Are you willing to have your pet neutered, and will you say so in writing? Will you take your dog to the vet regularly?

Rather than being offended by these questions, potential Golden owners should see them as a sign that the breeder really cares about his or her puppies and is breeding with the Golden Retriever's best interest in mind. That's a good thing because the puppies are likely to be beautiful, healthy, and have just the right temperament to make an excellent family pet. A breeder with a commitment to his or her dogs will most likely be a valuable resource for you and your Golden Retriever, so choose your breeder with care.

To find a breeder, you can check with your nearest Golden Retriever breed club who can refer you to breeders they know have the Golden Retriever's best interests at heart. Or, try asking your vet for the names of good Golden Retriever breeders. If you find a breeder through a newspaper ad, screen the breeder carefully to eliminate the possibility that the breeder is just breeding for profit (see the questions and checklists below). Even if it takes a while, finding a good breeder is worth every minute of your time. Here's the catch—sometimes it can be tricky to tell which Golden Retriever breeders are working to improve the breed and which are just breeding for profit. Does the breeder have the resources and knowledge to breed for good genetic health and temperament? How do you know the difference?

You interview the breeder, that's how. Ask the breeder lots of questions about Golden Retrievers, even if you already think you know the answer from your research. Here are some questions to get you started, as well as some sample answers you do and don't want to hear.

Questions to Ask a Golden Retriever Breeder

1. *What are your breeding priorities?*

   Good answer: I breed for good health, a sound structure, and that classic friendly, trainable Golden Retriever temperament. My dogs can do what Golden Retrievers were originally bred to do.

   Bad answer: Umm...I guess I hadn't really thought about that.

2. *Are you a member of any breed club?*

   Good answer: Oh yes, I am a member of a Golden Retriever breed club. Here is the web site and information on our club and what we do for Golden Retrievers.

   Bad answer: No, I'm very busy and I don't have time for clubs.

3. *What health tests have you done on the parents of the litter, and/*

Ask the breeder plenty of questions before you decide to take a puppy home.

A great place to find a show breeder is to contact a Golden Retriever Club (UK), which can refer you to show breeders in your area who have puppies available. Log on to www.thegoldenretrieverclub.co.uk

or the puppies? Can I see documentation of these tests?

Good answer: For the parents of the litter, I have had them checked for hip dysplasia, elbow dysplasia, eye disease, and heart defects. I have the results of all the tests, which you are welcome to see. I have also had both parents tested to check that they are free from heart murmurs or other indications of heart disease.

Bad answer: My lines don't have any genetic disease, so I don't feel testing is necessary.

4. *How soon can I take home a puppy after the litter is born?*

   Good answer: No sooner than 8 to 12 weeks. I want to make sure the puppies get the full benefit of nursing and time with their mother and littermates to help teach them good behaviour. This is an important part of socialising the new puppies.

   Bad answer: You can take the puppy home at five or six weeks, the sooner the better!

5. *What do you do to socialise the puppies before they go to their new homes?*

   Good answer: I raise the puppies inside the home, in the middle of the family. We handle the puppies gently every day, talk to them often, play with them, and help them begin housetraining. We have even taught some of the older puppies to sit, using bits of their dry food. We make sure they have already been exposed to children, our other dogs, and different adults, but we always make sure that exposure is fun and positive for the puppies, to help build their self-confidence and trust in humans.

   Bad answer: We go out to the kennel run every day and pet them when we give them their food. We let them out to run around together for a while every day. Is that what you mean?

6. *What kind of guarantees do you offer? Do I have to sign a contract?*

   Good answer: I have a contract that protects both of us. You agree to have the puppy checked by a vet within 48 hours to ensure the puppy is healthy when you take him home. If the vet finds anything wrong, you can bring the puppy back to me for a refund, or I will help you to find another puppy. If, later in life, your puppy develops a genetic disease, you can return the puppy to me for a full refund, or I will help you to pay for treatment of the disease. However, if the puppy develops a health problem or injury that is not genetic or is the result of anything that happens after you take the puppy home, this is your responsibility. If at any time during the dog's life you can no longer keep him, for whatever reasons, you must return him to me, no questions asked. I brought this

puppy into the world, so I am responsible for him and will always take him back any time, for any reason.
Bad answer: Look at this puppy; he is perfectly healthy. If a vet says he isn't, you can return him, but after 48 hours, he is your responsibility.

7. *What if I have any questions after I take the puppy home?*
Good answer: I am always available to answer your questions and help you with any problems. (Please be courteous about what time you call!) I can also point you to some excellent resources to help you handle typical Golden Retriever issues, including a good veterinary surgeon if you don't already have one, a good trainer who uses positive reinforcement methods, and a list of good books.
Bad answer: Just search "Golden Retriever" on the Internet, you'll find plenty of information. Please don't call me at home.

8. *Do I have to get the puppy spayed or castrated? What if I want to breed him or her?*
Good answer: Breeding dogs is a complicated, expensive, and time-consuming undertaking, and I strongly discourage anyone taking it lightly. If you want to become a Golden Retriever breeder, I can certainly point you in the right direction, so you can start learning about what is involved, but if you plan to breed "just for fun," I will not sell you a puppy. In my contract, I specifically require that you get the puppy neutered. There are already too many unwanted Golden Retrievers out there, and no serious breeder makes money breeding Golden Retrievers. It is just too expensive. However, if you are interested in a show-quality puppy and want to exhibit the dog in dog shows, we can discuss that option, and I can tell you all about what that involves. Bad answer: If you don't want to be stuck with a litter of puppies you can't sell, get the dog spayed or castrated, but of course the decision is up to you.

9. *Can you provide references?*
Good answer: Certainly. Here is the name and number of my veterinary surgeon. I can also arrange for you to talk to several people who have Golden Retrievers from me, but you will understand that I am not comfortable giving out their contact information. If you give me your phone number or e-mail, I will have them contact you.
Bad answer: I can't give out people's contact information. My puppies are healthy, so I haven't yet had to take them to the vet.

Keeping Records

Breeders should maintain careful records to keep everything legal and accountable, including the puppy's breed, sex, colour, date of birth, registered names and numbers of the puppy's parents (called the "sire" and the "dam"), and the name and address of the breeder. Do not work with a breeder who promises to send you this information later, after the purchase. You should receive all this information and paperwork when you receive the puppy.

Make sure you meet and observe the mother of the litter you are choosing from.

Good Breeder Checklist

You can learn a lot about a breeder just by paying attention. When you check out breeders, take this list with you to see if the breeder measures up. These are signs that you are probably dealing with a responsible, experienced, ethical breeder:

- The breeder interviews you just as intensely as you interview the breeder.
- The breeder keeps the puppies in the house, in the centre of the family, and family members handle the puppies often.
- The breeder insists that you have a fenced garden or are willing to provide the Golden Retriever with plenty of exercise, and asks

about your home situation and willingness to commit to caring for a Golden Retriever.

- The puppies look clean and healthy with shiny coats, bright eyes, and no bare patches or discharge from eyes, nose, ears, or rear.
- Both parents, or at least the mother of the litter, are available for you to see and interact with. The parents look and act the way you would want your own pet to look and act.
- The breeder's home is clean, with the signs of a dog-friendly home. (Pet hair expected!)
- The breeder is friendly and open, willing to answer any questions and provide references.
- The breeder doesn't just tell you the good things about Golden Retrievers, but also the challenging parts, to be sure you know what you are getting into.
- The breeder offers a health guarantee that protects you in case the puppy is ill or comes down with a genetic disease, in which case the breeder will replace the dog or help you pay for treatment.
- The breeder is always willing to take the dog back, throughout the dog's entire life, if you can't keep him for any reasons, and will insist that you return the dog rather than abandon or relinquish the dog to a rescue centre. Of course, if you give up the dog, the breeder should not be expected to refund your money.

How to Register Your Golden Retriever With the KC, AKC, or UKC

If you buy a Golden Retriever from a reputable breeder who has registered the parents with the Kennel Club, you will probably be eligible to register your dog with the Kennel Club (KC). Some breeders sell pets on a limited registration basis, meaning that the pet has to be neutered but can still be registered. Registered purebred dogs are eligible to compete in KC-sponsored events like conformation shows, obedience competition, and agility trials. Plus, your dog gets to have an official registered name that is unique. If you register your puppy with the Kennel Club, you can get six weeks of free pet health insurance. The breeder should register the litter with the Kennel Club (assuming the litter is eligible), then provide you with transfer of ownership papers with everything signed and ready for you to send in. When you send in this paperwork, ownership is transferred to you and the puppy is officially registered.

In the US, if you buy a puppy from a breeder who is a member of the the Golden Retriever Club of America, you will probably be able to register your dog with the American Kennel Club (AKC). To register your Golden Retriever, you should receive a blue slip from the breeder/seller. Fill out this blue slip, and send it to the American Kennel Club with the specified fee. The AKC will process this information and send you a registration certificate.

To register your puppy with the United Kennel Club (UKC), both parents must be UKC registered, and the puppy must be under one year old. Write or call the UKC to get an application. They also have other registration categories for dogs whose parents are registered with other registries (like the AKC), and a limited privilege application for dogs of unknown parentage or mixed breeds.

- The breeder is happy to be an ongoing resource of information and help for you as you work to raise your Golden Retriever puppy to be the best that he can be!

Adoption Options

Even though a good breeder is an excellent source for a Golden Retriever puppy, this option isn't for everyone. Some people feel better about adopting a Golden Retriever, especially when there are Golden Retrievers without homes (and that always seems to be the case, unfortunately). For people who prefer an adult dog, adopting a Golden Retriever from an all-breed rescue centre or Golden Retriever rescue group may be the perfect option (and sometimes these sources may also have puppies).

Rescue Centres

Adopting a Golden in need is a noble deed, but it also requires certain precautions and considerations. Rescue centres are likely to take some precautions of their own, to help reduce the chances that

Adopting a Golden in need of a home is a noble deed.

the dogs they adopt will end up right back at the centre. The first precaution will be to screen potential adopters. Some centres have a more rigorous process for this than others, depending on the way they are funded. In the UK, there are a number of large charities that run rescue centres in various locations. They include the Blue Cross (www.bluecross.org.uk), the RSPCA (www.rspca.org.uk), Dogs Trust (www.dogstrust.org.uk) and Battersea Dogs Home (www.dogshome.org).

Some rescue centres require consent from a landlord if you don't own your home. Some may refuse to adopt to students. Some may require a fenced garden, and many require that the dog be spayed or castrated before adoption, a service you will probably have to pay for (although many centres have agreements with local vets to reduce the cost of this service for centre animals). All of these requirements are for the good of the animal, and not designed to annoy you.

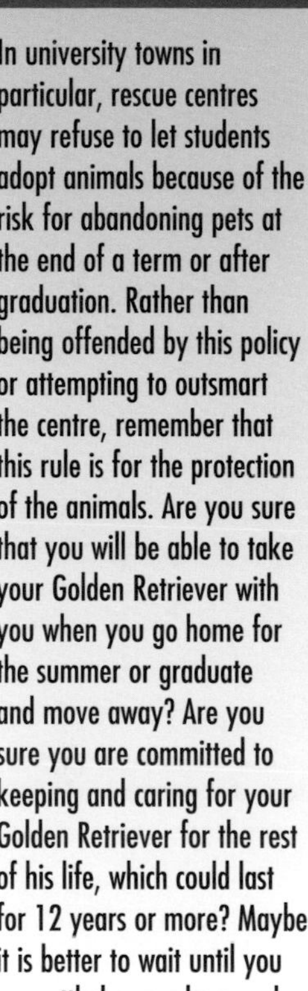

A Dog in Your Dorm?

In university towns in particular, rescue centres may refuse to let students adopt animals because of the risk for abandoning pets at the end of a term or after graduation. Rather than being offended by this policy or attempting to outsmart the centre, remember that this rule is for the protection of the animals. Are you sure that you will be able to take your Golden Retriever with you when you go home for the summer or graduate and move away? Are you sure you are committed to keeping and caring for your Golden Retriever for the rest of his life, which could last for 12 years or more? Maybe it is better to wait until you are settled somewhere and know you have the time and resources to commit to that awesome responsibility.

Rescues

Rescue groups work somewhat differently than rescue centres. These typically all-volunteer networks may work with any breed, but often stick exclusively to a single breed. A Golden Retriever rescue may be organised through a local or national breed club, or may be run independently by people who simply love and want to help any Golden Retriever left without a home.

When someone finds out about a Golden Retriever who needs a home, rescue workers will typically find volunteer foster care for the dogs in need, so the dog has somewhere to go while the rescue group searches for a good home. Rescue groups are also good at screening Goldens, because the foster home gets to know the dog and can help to determine whether the dog is comfortable with children and other pets, and whether the dog has any medical or behavioural problems. In many cases, the rescue workers and/or foster "parents" pay to have the dogs checked by a vet, pay to have any problems treated, and even pay for basic obedience classes, to increase the chances that the dog will find a good home.

Adopting a dog from a rescue group is a great way to help a needy Golden, but just as with a good breeder, expect to be grilled. Rescue workers see enough tragedy and don't want to send Goldens who have already been through loss and pain into another bad situation. Or, consider volunteering as a Golden Retriever foster home.

Puppy Proofing

The best way to puppy proof your home is to get down on your hands and knees and look at your home from your puppy's perspective.

What a great way to get to know Golden Retrievers before committing to full-time ownership.

GOLDEN-PROOF YOUR HOME

A Golden Retriever puppy is a little bit like a toddler—a toddler who sheds and has very sharp teeth! Just like a toddler, a Golden puppy can get into things that could be dangerous. Puppies can choke on small objects they put in their mouths. They can eat things that are poisonous for dogs, like chocolate, onions, antifreeze, human medications, or spoiled food. They can get into poisonous plants, they can chew wires and get electrocuted, or they can get stuck behind or inside furniture (watch out for that recliner!). As much as they like water, they could even drown in a swimming pool or just a large tub of water if they get in and can't get back out.

The best way to make your home safe for your new puppy, not to mention minimise destruction of your favourite belongings and furniture, is to thoroughly puppy-proof your home before bringing home the puppy. Here's how to do it:

- *Get down.* The best way to begin puppy-proofing your home is to get down on your hands and knees, at puppy level, and look around in any room your puppy would be. What do you see? Tasty chewy electrical wires? Tantalising fringe, tassels, or mini-blind cords to yank on? Delicate breakable objects? Try to get as many of these things as possible secured safely out of your puppy's reach.
- *Pick up.* Choking hazards like stray pieces of string, paperclips, or other small objects could pose a choking hazard. Pick up all small objects off the floor, and clear reachable surfaces.
- *Secure the space.* Secure easy-open low cabinets with safety latches to keep prying noses from opening them. Put rubbish behind closed doors. Install baby gates across open areas to block your puppy from places you don't want him to go.
- *Prepare for hair.* Remember, Golden Retrievers shed! Cover surfaces you don't want covered in pet hair with throw blankets and furniture covers. Do you have a good vacuum cleaner and some pet hairbrushes? Also consider changing your wardrobe to include more gold!
- *It's a chew fest!* Finally, never forget that Golden Retriever puppies chew...a lot! If you don't want your shoes, clothing, and

favourite pieces of furniture gnawed to bits, be ready to keep a steady supply of chewables available to your Golden Retriever puppy at all times. Set up a toy box with your Golden's toys, so he knows where to find the things he is allowed to chew. Keep your shoes and clothes put away, and encourage kids to keep their toys picked up. Nothing teaches a child to keep his room clean better than a Golden puppy who loves to destroy toys! Finally, you might need a spray-on chewing deterrent for furniture, baseboards, and other things you can't move out of reach that your puppy decides he wants to chew.

GOLDEN ESSENTIALS

Another important part of preparing your home for your new puppy is to have the right supplies. While you could spend hundreds of pounds on fancy puppy stuff, you can also get the basic supplies you need for much less. Here are the essential puppy supplies every new Golden Retriever owner should have on hand.

Food and Water Bowls

Choose bowls that are heavy and indestructible. Weighted metal or heavy ceramic won't tip as easily and won't tempt your Golden to chew like plastic bowls might. They are also easier to clean and less likely to collect bacteria.

Crate

This doggy "den" is essential for housetraining your new puppy, but a crate does more than teach your puppy when it is and is not appropriate to "go toilet." Dogs are den animals and a crate provides your dog with a secure, safe space for when he needs to get away from the stimulation and excitement of his new home. He can use it for napping, for gnawing a nice chew toy, or as a place to enjoy some downtime whenever things get too hectic. Train your puppy right and he will come to love and cherish his "den."

Wire and plastic crates are both acceptable options, but dogs like an enclosed den and feel safest in their dens if they are only exposed on one side. If confined to a small space but exposed on all sides, dogs can get anxious. Plastic crates are already like this, making them preferable to some. You can even buy ones that fold away for easy storage. Others like the look or portability of a wire

Puppies should not be taken away from their mother before eight weeks of age.

cage better, but if you choose this type, cover the top, sides, and back of a wire crate with a blanket or, when outside, with a waterproof cover. This keeps the sun off and gives your dog—inside or outside—a safe, secure feeling.

Lead and Collar

Every dog needs to learn how to walk on a lead. If you take your Golden out in urban areas, he needs to be safe—especially when he sees a squirrel on the other side of the busy road. Leads and collars are also a huge help when it comes to training. A light nylon collar and 6-foot lead are appropriate for puppies, but adults can use them too. Nylon leads and collars are wash-

able, and you can buy reflective kinds, which are better for walking dogs at night. Leather leads are easier to grip, less likely to chafe your skin if your dog is pulling at the lead, and develop a lovely patina as they age. Both last long with proper care, so it really depends on your preference. Leads and collars come in many different styles and collars, from basic utilitarian to crystal encrusted, leather studded with metal, lighted and flashing, or with logos of your favourite sports team, cartoon character, or celebrity.

Retractable leads are good options when walking in areas where you want to allow your dog to explore off the path, but they aren't a good idea if you are trying to teach your dog to heel and not to pull on the lead. If this isn't a problem, a retractable lead works fine. Just be sure you are still able to keep control of your dog if necessary.

Premium Food

Doesn't your Golden Retriever deserve quality nutrition? Spend a little more for the premium or super-premium brand of food, and you'll not only be delivering better nutrition but you'll decrease your dog's stool volume, which makes cleaning up after him a much more pleasant experience.

Identification Tags

Every dog should wear identification, just in case. If your Golden gets lost and somebody finds him, all it will take to return him to you is a phone call. Keep those tags on at all times! If you can't stand that jingly noise, get the kind of tags that are riveted right onto the collar.

Other Forms of Identification

If your Golden wanders away, slips his lead, escapes from an open fence gate, or runs out the front door, an identification tag

Checklist for Your Golden

- Food and Water Bowls
- Crate
- Lead and Collar
- ID Tags
- Toys

can help him find his way back home by providing contact information for good Samaritans who may find him. But sometimes, an identification tag isn't enough. Tags can get lost, fall off, or a Golden can lose his collar. Or (and this happens a lot), you might have taken off that collar for any number of reasons: the irritating noise of the jingling tags, switching to a different collar and forgetting to switch the tags, or because you thought your Golden would be more comfortable without it.

Fortunately, there are other back-up methods of identification that every Golden Retriever owner may consider. Microchipping is one handy method of identification. A tiny chip is implanted in dog's skin, usually in the flesh area over his shoulders. It contains contact information for your dog: your own details, and in some cases, the vet's contact information.

Many people have successfully recovered their dogs, thanks to microchips. This isn't a perfect system, however. You must fill out and send in registration papers, so the microchip company can enter your dog's information in its national database. If you fail to do this, the microchip manufacturer's name and ID number on the chip will be meaningless. Furthermore, because several different companies manufacture microchips, not every scanner can read every microchip. If your vet or rescue centre has a scanner for one chip and your dog has another chip, the scanner won't see it.

Still, microchips are an effective identification mechanism, and more vets and rescue centres have scanners. The best way to ensure that a microchip will do the job is to call your local rescue centre or vet and ask which kind of scanner they use, so you can buy the correct microchip. This shouldn't be difficult because in most cases, the centre where you adopted your dog or the vet where you take your dog will implant the chip for you.

Other identification methods, like tattooing and registering your dog with online services, can also help to identify your pet if he gets lost. Your first line of defense, however, is to keep those ID tags on… at all times! (If the jingling bothers you, get one of those tags that is riveted to the collar, or one of the colourful "tag bags" that keep all the tags together, safely cushioned, on the collar in a little sack.)

Toys, Toys, Toys

Toys aren't just a luxury. For a puppy, they encourage play, learning, interaction, and best of all, an opportunity to chew something

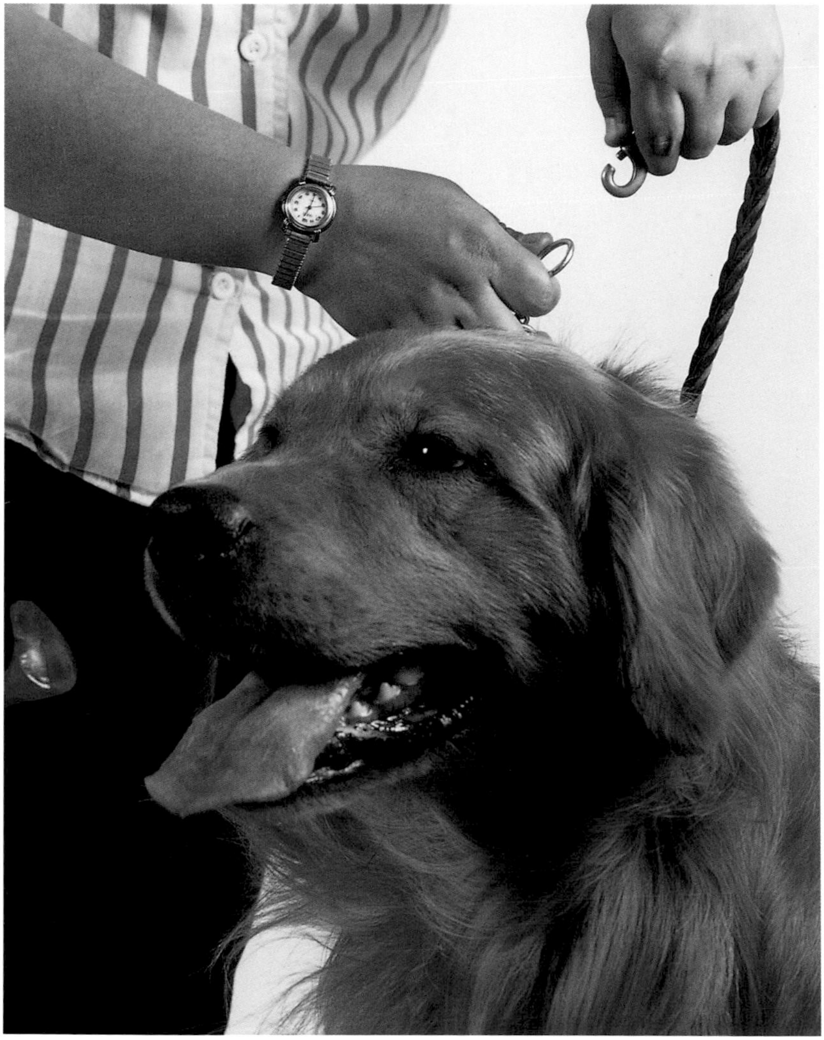

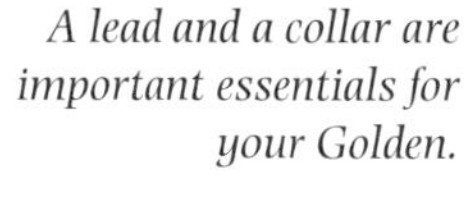

A lead and a collar are important essentials for your Golden.

appropriate. Remember how much Goldens need to chew! Golden Retrievers will quickly learn which toys are theirs if you give them their own toy box—a simple box or laundry basket will do. Keep it full of interesting toys, and rotate the toys every week or two so your Golden doesn't get bored with the same old toys and will always find something new and different in that basket. If you don't want your Golden to chew your children's stuffed animals, avoid giving stuffed toys. Goldens typically enjoy balls, Frisbees, Nylabones, and anything and everything appropriate for gnawing. Also try stuffable toys you can fill with treats, especially those that make your Golden work to get the treats out. This will keep your Golden's mind as well as his teeth occupied for hours.

Goldens love to chew, so make sure you provide them with something appropriate to chew on.

Golden Luxuries

Here are some of the luxury items you might want to buy your Golden, just for fun.

Gourmet Treats

You can always use bits of dry food and healthy "people" food for training, and some Goldens are happiest with tiny bits of hot dogs or cheese for training motivation, but some Goldens just love fancy doggy treats. Don't feed these too often, or you could risk contributing to a weight problem (one of the most common health problems in Golden Retrievers, according to vets). However, as an occasional special reward, treats are fun. A number of pet superstores are now offering a wide variety of gourmet treats, and many smaller pet stores offer gourmet treats, too. Gourmet treat packages make nice gifts for dogs, too.

Fancy Furniture

Does your Golden Retriever need an expensive dog bed? A chaise lounge? A velvet throw? A special ramp to help him get out of the swimming pool more easily? His own upholstered couch? Probably not. That doesn't mean you can't buy them, if you want to! Many people like the idea of spoiling their Golden—just a little—and much of the fancy furniture available today can look great in your home.

Canine Couture

You look stunning in your satin jacket, dah-ling! While sweaters, jackets, coats, jaunty berets, doggy boots, and other canine costumes have traditionally been reserved for smaller dogs, more and more manufacturers are meeting the fashion needs of larger breeds. Also, look for holiday-themed dress-up ware, from angel wings and halos for Christmas to devil horns and pumpkin suits for Halloween. Jewellery, too? You bet! Canine necklaces made with crystals and charms look stunning on a beautiful Golden.

WHEN YOU GO AWAY

Whether you go to work every day, or leave on holiday for a month, your Golden Retriever would rather go with you than be left at home. If you can take your Golden Retriever to work, every-

You can provide your Golden with some fun furniture of his own to play on.

On the Road Again

- If you decide to take your Golden Retriever on the road with you, be prepared. Here's what to remember:
- Whether hotels, campgrounds, or friends' houses, call ahead to confirm the places you will be staying allow dogs.
- Be courteous and respectful of others, wherever you go. Always clean up after your dog.
- Don't forget the lead, collar, and identification tags. Keep tags on at all times, and be sure the identification information is complete and accurate, including area code.
- Bring food and water bowls, and a supply of your dog's regular food, and a few jugs of the same water you normally give your dog (out of your tap, for example).
- Chew toys and other comforting items in your dog's crate will help him feel more secure. Of course, don't forget the crate!
- Always use a doggy seatbelt in the car, in case of a car accident. This will help to protect your dog and the other passengers in your car.
- Dogs are creatures of habit, and some dogs can get very stressed by changes in routine. Stay alert and aware of how your dog is doing. If he gets scared and needs reassurance, or is getting hyperactive, be ready to take control before the behaviour gets out of hand.
- Bring an emergency first-aid kit including bandages, disinfectant, antibiotic cream, steroid cream, Benadryl, any medications your dog requires, grooming equipment, a blanket, a safe pest control product, doggy sunscreen and/or other protective gear, and anything else your vet recommends. Also include a card with your vet's name, address, and phone number (these things are easy to forget when you are flustered), and the number of a 24-hour emergency clinic. Also, ask your vet ahead of time for any dosing information, just in case. (For example, if your dog gets an allergic reaction, how much Benadryl should he take?)

one is happy! If you can travel with your Golden on holiday, great! Golden Retrievers make good travel companions, and can quickly learn to ride in the car—in a doggy seatbelt or crate of course, for everyone's safety—and to behave nicely at rest stops and even in hotels, motels, and campgrounds that allow dogs (more and more of them do these days, but call ahead to make sure).

If you can't take your Golden Retriever with you, however, you have a lot of options for care. Many people make their living from dog sitting, or from boarding dogs. Gone are the days when your only option was to stick your dog in a tiny kennel at a boarding facility where he had to sit for days or weeks until you got back, with only a few chances to get out each day.

Check with your vet about local options for care. Home boarding, where dogs are kept in the carer's own home, is a popular choice, but you will need to check out, interview, and get references for anyone you plan to employ. Services aren't all the same, and cheaper often isn't better. Your Golden deserves careful and complete care when you are away!

Boarding Kennels

Modern boarding facilities often are located on farms or have large play areas, with opportunities for dogs to get lots of playtime and socialisation, special attention, even spa-like pampering services like fancy treats, pet massage, and lots of individual attention. If you opt for boarding kennels, always check the facilities and find out how many dogs are boarded at a time.

Pet Sitting

Pet sitting is another option. Professional pet sitters will visit your house, walk your dog, clean the waste from your garden, even stay overnight in your house, take in your mail, feed your fish, and water your plants. Some are pricey, but then again, your dog never has to leave his comfortable and familiar surroundings.

Pet Sitters International, a trade organisation for professional pet sitters, has provided this list of what to look for in a professional pet sitter. (Most of these also apply to what to look for in a boarding kennel.)

- The sitter is insured.
- The sitter provides references.

You can bring your Golden on the road with you, as long as you take some simple precautions.

- The sitter has adequate knowledge and experience in caring for pets and is clearly mindful of their safety and well-being.
- The sitter provides written literature describing services and stating fees.
- The sitter visits the client's home before the first pet sitting assignment to meet the pets and get detailed information about their care.
- The sitter shows a positive attitude during the initial meeting and seems comfortable and competent dealing with animals.
- The sitter wants to learn as much as possible about the animals in his or her care.
- The sitter provides a service contract that specifies services and fees.
- The sitter is courteous, interested and well informed.
- The sitter keeps regular office hours and answers client inquiries and complaints promptly.
- The sitter provides a service rating form for clients.
- The sitter takes precautions to make sure a client's absence from home is not detected because of any careless actions or disclosures made by the sitter.
- The sitter conducts business with honesty and integrity and observes all legal requirements pertaining to business operations and animal care.
- The sitter has a contingency plan for pet care in case of inclement weather or personal illness.
- The sitting service screens applicants for employment carefully.
- The sitter calls to confirm or has the client call to confirm the client has returned home.

Air Travel

Travelling in an aeroplane with your dog has its pros and cons. While you might hear occasional stories in the news about dogs exposed to extreme temperatures or dogs that got loose in the cargo area, travelling by air with your dog is usually safe, and many people do it. People with large dogs like Golden Retrievers often choose to travel with their dogs by car instead, but sometimes air travel is necessary.

To travel by air, dogs must travel in the cargo area in their kennels, and you will have to pay an additional fee to travel with a dog, up to several hundred pounds. (Only small dogs, cats, and other small animals can travel in the cabin with you.) Crates must be approved by the airline, and airlines may have a limit on how many animals they will take per flight, so book your flight early and tell them in advance that you are bringing a dog. Every airline has different rules, so find out when you book your flight exactly what the crate requirements are and what kind of documentation you need. You might have to prove your dog is current on vaccinations, especially rabies, and you may have to have a health certificate from a vet.

- The sitter refrains from criticising competitors.
- The sitting service provides initial and ongoing training for its sitters.
- The sitter exhibits courtesy and professionalism in all dealings with staff members, customers and industry colleagues so as to present the pet sitter and the pet sitting industry favourably and positively.

Pet Travel Scheme (PETS)

PETS is a system that permits companion animals from certain countries to travel to the UK without undergoing a period of quarantine. This scheme also applies to people in the UK who want to travel with their pets to other European Union countries.

For more information, visit the Department for Environment Food and Rural Affairs' web site at www.defra.gov.uk.

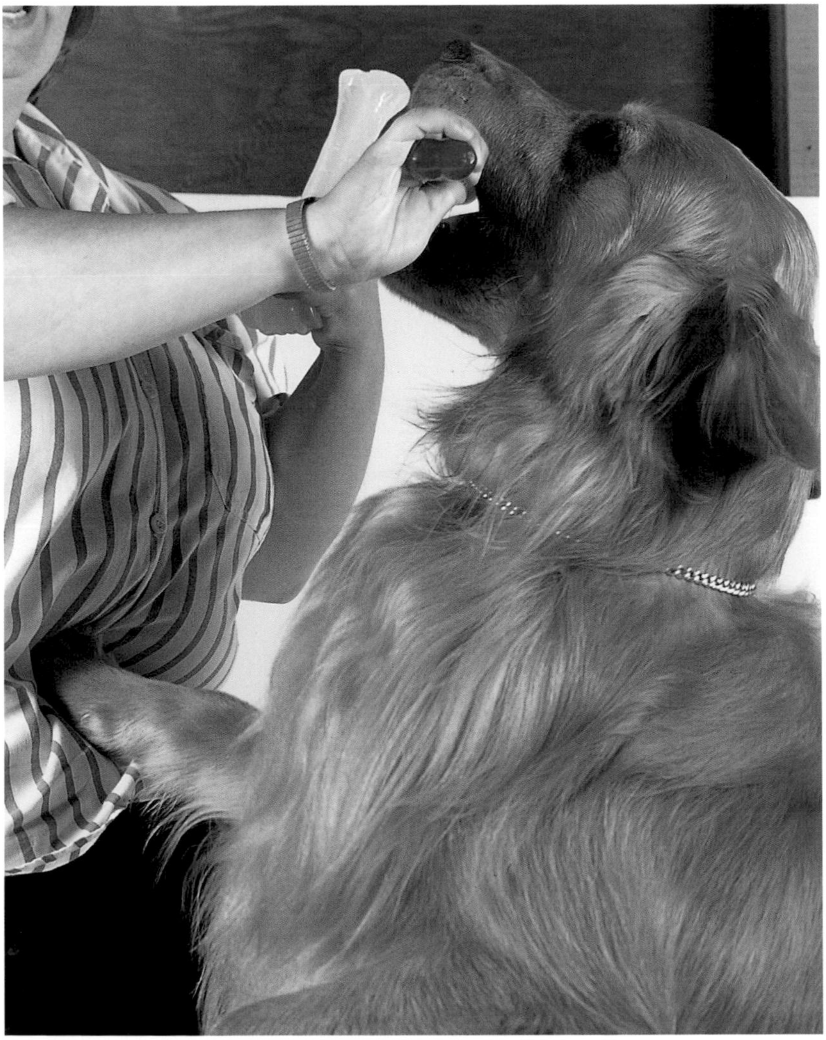

If you can't bring your Golden Retriever with you when you travel, make sure you find someone trustworthy to care for him.

Chapter 4

FEEDING

Your Golden Retriever

Golden Retrievers may be products of their breeding, socialisation, and training, but they are also products of their diets. What you feed your Golden Retriever can have a big impact on his future health, but take a look at the pet store shelf of dog food and you might just feel a little overwhelmed. Didn't feeding a dog used to be easy? You just grabbed a bag or a can and that was that. Today, the options are mind boggling: dry food for every breed, size, and heath condition; canned food, from the supermarket variety to high-end natural options; frozen raw food stored in the pet store's freezer; or maybe you should make a homemade diet for your Golden Retriever?

Feeding a Golden Retriever is easy, but feeding your pet a nutritious diet best suited for this breed's size and health profile is a little more difficult. As a pet owner, you can actually help to prevent some of the health conditions Golden Retrievers tend to develop by feeding your Golden the right diet, and practicing certain lifestyle changes. You just need a little knowledge first, and everything you need to know, you'll find in this chapter.

DOG FOOD BEGINNINGS

Once upon a time, dog food didn't exist. Can you imagine? When dogs and humans first got together, the tamer dogs would get closer and accept people's leftover food. When dogs became domesticated, people fed their pets the leftover scraps from their dinner plates, their campfire cast-offs, and whatever else just wasn't going to get eaten. And the dogs got by just fine. Or did they? Actually, dogs lived shorter lives in the pre dog-diet days, partially because of diseases like distemper that are now largely under control because of vaccinations, partly because veterinary care wasn't as advanced as it is today, and partly—or so many vets believe—because they didn't get adequate nutrition. Because life for dogs was so different a century ago, it is difficult to

Frozen Raw Food

A recent trend in dog food is frozen raw diets made with raw meat and ground vegetables. Just purchase them from your local pet store, store them in the freezer, then defrost and serve.

determine for sure how much dietary changes have influenced pet health, and the subject is quite controversial. Some people think dogs were healthier before the advent of commercial pet food (for more on this, see later section in this chapter about homemade diets).

Commercial Dog Food

An American living in England essentially invented commercial dog food by baking up biscuits of wheat meal, meat, and vegetables. In the early twentieth century, customers could find some bulk dry dog foods made from meal and pellets, but they barely resembled the dry dog food in stores today. Around this time, canned dog food also debuted, made from horsemeat.

Further developments came in the 1950s, when Purina invented extrusion, launching a whole new era of pet food. In the 1960s, semimoist food was invented, and in the 1970s, the Iams Company and Hills Science Diet began producing premium foods with superior nutrient profiles.

Other companies quickly followed suit. Dry dog food got more and more nutritious, and more and more expensive. The 1990s brought specialisation to the market and consumers began to see more and more dog foods designed for highly specific dogs and their highly specific conditions. Food for giant breeds, toy breeds, working dogs, and canine athletes cozied up to foods for puppies, adults, senior dogs, and overweight dogs. Then so-called natural foods, organic foods, and foods made with human-grade ingredients began to proliferate.

Nutritional Requirements in Commercial Foods

Of course, every pet food manufacturer can tell you why that particular brand of food is best for dogs, and often why another type of food isn't so good. Dry food, canned food, natural food, raw diets, even prescription foods for certain conditions all have a place and can all be appropriate, depending on the dog and the owner. So, what's a well-meaning Golden owner to do? Should you just close your eyes and pick one?

In the UK, pet food is controlled by the Food Standards Agency (FSA), which has to adhere to EC guidelines. Manufacturers also belong to the Pet Food Manufacturer's Association (PFMA), which, in turn, follows guidelines laid down by the European

Pet Food Industry Federation (FEDIAF). Every label contains the following information:

- Ingredients list
- Additives (preservatives, colourings, etc.)
- Vitamins
- Best before date
- Bar code
- Batch number
- Net weight
- Name and address.

Going Beyond the Minimum Requirements

The nutritional standards stated in law and given on pet food labels are only minimum requirements. Do you want your Golden to subsist, or do you want your Golden's food to go above and beyond the minimum requirement for avoiding malnutrition?

Your growing puppy needs proper nutrition for his life stage.

Foods Toxic for Goldens (and All Dogs!)

Never feed these foods to your Golden—they are poisonous to dogs:

- Onions
- Chocolate, especially dark chocolate
- Grapes and raisins
- Spoiled food (if you wouldn't eat it, don't give it to your dog)

Many premium foods include ingredients that may add valuable phytochemicals (nonnutritive plant substances that may have important disease-fighting effects). Many are customised for very specific situations, like dogs with arthritis or for large breeds. You need to find out what is the best choice for your Golden.

That means you must also know your Golden and the nutrients he needs for his life stage. Is he a growing puppy? Maybe a puppy food isn't the best choice because Goldens need to grow slowly for proper bone density. Or, maybe a puppy food custom formulated for slow bone growth in puppies is the best choice. Does your Golden have sensitive skin? He may need a unique protein source like a fish-based food, with its omega-3 fatty acids and non-allergenic salmon.

You aren't alone in making a decision about the best food for your dog. Talk to your vet or breeder about your concerns if you want help choosing the food that will help your Golden grow strong bones, supple skin, and a shiny soft coat. Food can help to keep your Golden in a state of glowing health through his adult years, and best meet his needs as a veteran.

But first, let's consider the different kinds of dog foods available to you.

TYPES OF DOG FOOD

Today, you can feed your dog any of several different types of dog food: dry food, wet canned food, semimoist food, a commercially prepared frozen raw diet, a homemade "Bones And Raw Food" (BARF) diet, a homemade cooked diet, or a combination of these, such as dry food mixed with canned food or dry food mixed with homemade cooked food. Let's take a closer look at each of these types, to get a better idea of what they are and what they can provide for your dog.

Dry Food

This is the most common type of dog food, but the premium and super-premium brands of dry food available today are far superior to the dry food available a decade ago.

The manufacturing process is largely the same. While a few specialty foods are baked rather than extruded, extrusion is generally the most efficient and cost-effective manufacturing process for dry food. Ingredients like meat and grains are combined, cooked, then forced under high pressure through an extruder to form noodle-like shapes that can then be sliced or formed into dry food of various sizes. The food is then dried, coated with supplemental ingredients like vitamins, minerals, preserving oils, and nutraceuticals (like probiotics to aid in digestion and glucosamine to support healthy joints), then packaged in a bag and shipped off to pet stores and supermarkets.

Food + Water

Adding water to dry food can make it easier for small puppies to chew and digest. Warm water can make dry food more palatable for some dogs, too. Some evidence suggests that dogs may be less likely to inhale wet food, reducing the potential for choking or swallowing too much air while eating.

The difference between dry food in the twenty-first century and the dry food of just a few decades ago has to do with the ingredients that go into the mix. Veterinary nutritional science has discovered a lot about what dogs need, not just to maintain an illness-free baseline, but to thrive at their healthy best. While you can still buy inexpensive dry food with low-quality ingredients, this is akin to feeding your children a diet of junk food. Sure, they might survive on it, but they will probably begin to suffer health problems. Many Goldens fed a poor diet gain too much weight, have loose, smelly stools, and suffer from itchy skin, a dull coat, and low energy.

Fortunately, premium foods have changed all that, and if you choose to feed your Golden Retriever dry food, you will probably find that the cost of premium food is well worth it. Using high quality ingredients designed for maximum health, these foods result in better health, and because they are more nutritionally dense, dogs don't need to eat as much of them. You'll also find it is much more pleasant picking up after Goldens—in the garden or on walks—if they are eating a premium diet.

Premium dry food typically contains meat and/or meat meal (meat meal is meat with all the moisture removed) as the first ingredient. Common choices include chicken, beef, and lamb, but you can also find formulas made with fish and venison. Because ingredients on the label are listed in order according to how

Dry Food

Dry Food Pros

- Convenient
- Long shelf life
- Many are nutritionally complete, requiring no supplementation
- Available in a wide variety of formulas
- Many vet-recommended premium brands
- Hard surface may help clean teeth

Dry Food Cons

- Low water content means dogs must also drink plenty of water
- Processing destroys nutrients that then must be added back in, resulting in a more processed food
- Some dogs don't like the taste

much the food contains, a food listing meat first means the food has more meat than any other ingredient. Because most dogs need high-quality meat protein in their diets, foods listing meat first are good choices for Goldens.

Premium dry food also typically contains grains like rice, oats, barley, wheat, soyabeans (not really a grain but often used in pet foods), and corn. Some dogs have trouble digesting corn, soya, and/or wheat, or may have allergic reactions to these grains. Premium dry food may also contain organ meats, eggs, and dairy products (like cottage cheese), animal and/or vegetable fat, fresh or dried vegetables (like carrots and kale), fresh or dried fruits (like blueberries, cranberries, and apples). They might also contain various other ingredients like nuts, seeds (including the omega-3-rich flaxseed), vegetable and nut oils, and supplemental ingredients such as vitamins, minerals, preservatives (often vitamin E oil), probiotics (like the friendly bacteria in yogurt), and nutraceuticals like glucosamine for joint health. Look for food that contains ingredients whose names you recognise, or with explanations of ingredients you don't recognise.

Dry food comes in bags and stays fresh for about a month, but can turn stale if exposed to air, and dogs (not to mention any stray creatures in the house from ants to rats) could easily tear through the paper bag for a nibble. Keep dry food in a plastic container with a tight-fitting lid, and only buy as much as your Golden Retriever will eat in two to three weeks. Few food choices can beat dry food for convenience, and most Golden Retrievers will happily devour their dry food. Veterinary surgeons generally recommend this type of food for Golden Retrievers.

Canned Food

Canned Food Pros

- Dogs often prefer the taste to dried food
- High water content helps hydrate dogs
- Many are nutritionally complete, requiring no supplementation
- Available in a wide variety of formulas
- Many vet-recommended premium brands
- When added to dry food, can make the diet more palatable

Canned Food Cons

- Once opened, short shelf life
- More expensive
- Not as nutritionally dense, so larger dogs have to eat large amounts to get enough nutrition
- Lower fibre could result in loose stools
- Some dogs don't like the taste, especially if they are used to dry food
- Some vets think canned food promotes tooth decay

Canned Dog Food

Canned dog food looks a lot more like meat than a scoop of dry food, and dogs often love the taste. Canned food is mixed, cooked, and canned without the moisture being removed, so the percentages on the can label look a lot different than the percentages on the bag of dry food. The percentage of protein in a dry food, for example, looks much higher than in a canned food, because the canned food has so much water. If a food is 90 percent water, then the remaining 10 percent of the food contains the part that has the nutrition, so this skews the percentages. To accurately compare, you have to do a little maths, but in general, canned food generally has higher protein.

Semimoist Food

Semimoist Food Pros

- Dogs often like the taste
- Many are nutritionally complete

Semimoist Food Cons

- Highly processed
- Contains artificial colours
- Contains higher amount of sugar
- Some vets think semimoist food promotes tooth decay

Most vets don't recommend canned food for large dogs like Goldens as the sole source of food. Not only would this be expensive, but dry food is nutritionally denser than canned food, so your dog doesn't have to eat as much to get the nutrition he needs. Many dogs enjoy a big spoonful of canned food mixed into their dryfood, however. Like dryfood, canned dog food comes in a wide variety of economical, premium, and super-premium brands. Also, like dryfood, the premium and super-premium varieties typically use higher quality ingredients and are probably worth the higher price.

Semimoist Food

Semimoist foods look like dry food but are softer. Generally, this type of food is highly processed, containing artificial colours and more sugar than Golden Retrievers should probably eat. Many dogs like the taste of semimoist food, but that doesn't mean they should eat it on a regular basis.

Raw Diet Food

Raw Diet Pros

- Dogs often like the taste
- Closer to the wild canine's natural diet
- Bones and raw meat may keep teeth and jaws strong and healthy
- Anecdotal evidence suggests raw diets resolve chronic health problems in some dogs
- Some vets think this is the ideal and most healthy diet for dogs
- Frozen prepared raw diets are convenient

Raw Diet Cons

- Raw meat contains bacteria that could cause illness in dogs or humans handling the meat
- Possible danger from ingesting bone fragments if bones are included
- Inconvenient to prepare from scratch
- Some vets think raw diets aren't good for dogs

Frozen Raw Diet/BARF Diet

Raw diets consist of raw meat, uncooked bones, ground vegetables and fruits, and sometimes cooked

whole grains like rice or oatmeal. Some people, including many holistic vets, strongly believe that dogs will be much healthier on a diet closer to what they once ate in the wild. When dogs had to fend for themselves, they would typically eat small animals, including their meat, organs, bones, and stomach contents (which typically included digested plant food). A bowl of dry food doesn't look much like a rabbit or a chicken.

Homemade Food

Homemade Cooked Diet Pros

- Dogs often like the taste
- Diet is less processed than dry food or canned food
- Some people find that preparing a home cooked diet for their dogs is very satisfying, and they feel closer to their pets
- If you cook healthy meals for yourself, you can simply share them with your dog rather than cooking a separate meal
- Closer to the wild canine's natural diet than processed dry food or canned food
- Dogs get to enjoy a wider variety of foods
- Could cost less than commercially prepared pet food, depending on what you cook
- Some vets think this is the ideal and healthiest diet for dogs

Homemade Cooked Diet Cons

- Cooking for your dog can be inconvenient and time consuming
- If your dog can't eat what you eat, you have to cook twice
- Some vets think homemade cooked diets can cause nutritional deficiencies in dogs

A raw meat diet must be carefully formulated to include all the necessary nutrients. A meat-only diet will quickly result in serious nutritional deficiencies! But proponents of the raw diet say that raw meat and raw bone are the foods nature intended for dogs to eat, that their digestive tracts are designed to handle the bacteria in raw meat, and that dogs on this diet thrive and are generally the picture of health. The bones keep dogs' teeth healthy and provide necessary minerals. The vegetables and grains provide necessary fibre.

But raw meat diets are controversial. Some vets believe the potential for food-borne illness is too great and that raw meat, in the state it is available today, just isn't good for dogs. They also worry about the dangers of ingesting bone fragments, if raw bones are included (never feed a dog any cooked bone, as these splinter easily and could cause internal damage).

Other vets believe commercially prepared pet food is far more dangerous, and the root of many chronic diseases in dogs today, such as allergies, cancer, even chronic behavioural problems. This is a sensitive subject and you can get ten different opinions from ten different veterinary surgeons.

The problem with raw diets, even for those who think they are the ideal diet for dogs, is that some people may find them unpleasant to prepare. Plus, the constant contact with raw meat can be a health hazard for humans, especially children. Enter the commercially prepared frozen raw diet! These convenient products eliminate the mess and guesswork from feeding a raw diet. Pet stores specialising in holistic/natural products often stock raw diets, which are kept in the freezer. Just defrost and serve.

Homemade Cooked Diet

For people who want to provide a homemade diet for their dogs but aren't comfortable with the whole raw concept, the homemade cooked diet may be just the ticket. Many people cook for their dogs, usually combining meat (such as chicken, turkey, beef, or fish) and chopped vegetables with rice, oatmeal, or barley. This might sound like a complicated nutritional balancing act, but if a dog's diet consists of a wide variety of healthy meats, cooked grains, and chopped vegetables, plus other healthy additions like plain yogurt, cottage cheese, eggs, and chopped fruits, the nutrition will take care of itself. Just avoid unhealthy and unsafe foods like onions, chocolate, excessive sugar, and processed food; include some raw crunchy vegetables for good dental health, such as baby carrots and broccoli florets. It's simple common sense, but you still may want to consult professional resources before cooking for your dog, to be sure you add all the right supplements. Talk to your breeder or vet if you are considering a homemade cooked diet, to be sure you are giving your dog everything he needs.

Combination Diets

The combination diet may be the most realistic option for people who want to feed their Goldens the healthiest possible diet, but don't always have the time or resources to cook for their pets or prepare raw diets. Combination diets can include a small amount of dry food mixed with canned food or raw meat and vegetables, or a primarily home-cooked or raw meat diet with the occasional addition of dry food or canned food when home-prepared diets aren't practical (such as when the owner is away). Just be sure

Combination Diet

Combination Diet Pros

- Get the benefits of commercial pet food and homemade diets in one
- Flexible
- Dogs get the benefit of a variety of nutrients
- Dogs often like the taste

Combination Diet Cons

- Some vets think you shouldn't add "people food" to your dog's commercial pet food diet
- Some vets think you shouldn't add commercial pet food to your dog's homemade diet
- Risk of nutritional deficiencies if diet isn't complete

your dog is getting a complete diet with protein, carbohydrates, fat, vitamins, and minerals. If you are unsure about the best food combination for your Golden, talk to your vet.

FEED BY BREED: GOLDEN CONCERNS AND FEEDING SCHEDULES

Some of the discussion previous to this point can be applied to dogs in general, but what about your Golden Retriever in particular? Once you've settled on a dietary strategy, you still have to think about how often and how much you need to feed your Golden, and which varieties of foods within a certain brand to choose. All these factors depend on your Golden's life stage (puppy, adult, veteran) as well as on your individual preferences. Some vets recommend feeding a set amount several times per day. For Goldens, look on the pet food label and start by feeding an amount on the lower end of the recommended range for your dog's age. For example, if the food says to feed 1 to 2 cups daily, start with 1 cup. If you are feeding several times per day, divide that amount by the number of feedings. Some vets recommend feeding as much as a puppy will eat in a set amount of time, such as ten minutes, then taking the food away. Ask your vet which method he or she recommends for your Golden.

Feeding a Golden Puppy

Puppies grow fast and burn a lot of energy, but that doesn't mean they need huge amounts of food. The slower a puppy grows, the healthier and denser his bones and joints will be as an adult. Some breeders and vets recommend feeding Golden puppies a premium adult diet from the beginning, rather than a puppy food. Or, look for a puppy food for large breed dogs specifically designed to slow bone growth. Avoid puppy foods that are high in fat, and avoid any dietary supplements with added calcium.

Vegetarian Dogs?

Most dogs should get their protein from high-quailty meat, but there are vegetarian dog food formulas available for those rare dogs that can't eat meat due to allergies or other health problems.

Puppies have quick metabolisms, so they can benefit from several smaller meals each day rather than one large meal. This keeps them more satisfied, gives them an exciting event (mealtime!) more than once a day, and avoids the frantic food gulping that could be associated with deadly bloat (gastric torsion). Feed puppies three times per day at least until six months, at which time you can decrease the number of feedings to twice a day. Or, keep feeding three times per day until the end of the first year, if desired. Your puppy will probably

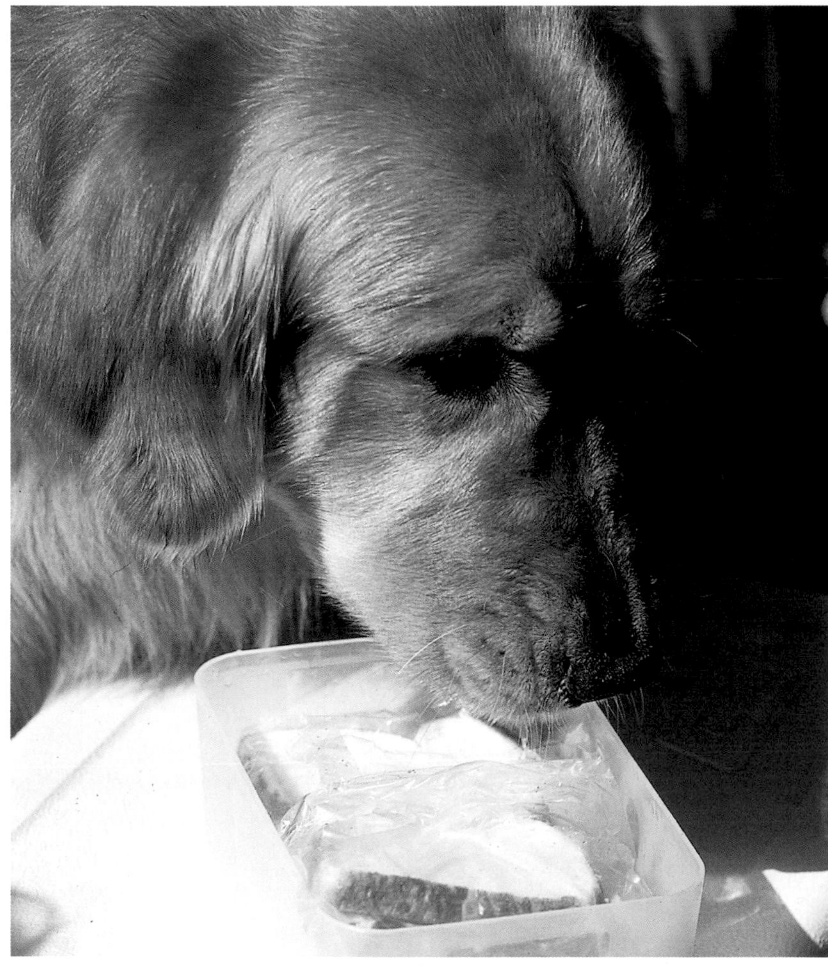

If you feed your Golden a homemade diet, make sure you avoid unhealthy or unsafe foods.

enjoy it. Just be sure you are dividing the daily food allowance by three, rather than overfeeding your Golden.

It is extremely important to bear in mind that a slim, trim Golden Retriever will have better bone growth and less stress on a fast-maturing body.

Feeding an Adult Golden

Adult dogs may benefit from being fed twice per day instead of just once. Some evidence suggests that multiple smaller meals are less likely than one large meal to contribute to bloat or gastric torsion, a life-threatening condition usually seen in larger breeds in which the stomach fills with gas and twists.

Feed adult Goldens a high-quality, premium food and continually monitor your adult for weight gain. Goldens who stay

Puppies have quick metabolisms, so they can benefit from several smaller meals each day rather than one large meal.

at a healthy weight throughout adulthood put much less strain on their bones and joints, minimising the effects of painful arthritis later in life. Slim Goldens are also less likely to suffer from a variety of chronic diseases and wear and tear on internal organs.

Feeding the Older Golden

Goldens usually reach veteran status around six or seven years old. Senior Goldens often suffer from degenerative joint disease and arthritis pain. A food containing joint-supporting ingredients like glucosamine and chondroitin could possibly offer some relief. Joint-support supplements designed for dogs may be an even more effective therapy because they offer higher dosages.

The notion that senior dogs need lower protein is not true. Veteran dogs need just as much protein as adult dogs, unless they are having kidney problems, in which case a prescription low-protein diet is appropriate. If your older dog remains active, you may not need to switch to a different food at all. If your dog does begin to slow down, however, and isn't happy with a reduced amount of food, a veteran food formula may be appropriate.

SUPPLEMENTATION AND SPECIAL DIETS

Many prescription diets now available for dogs are formulated to address chronic diseases. You can find foods designed to address allergies, digestive problems, food intolerance, kidney disease and urinary tract problems, liver disease, heart disease, diabetes, and even canine cognitive dysfunction (an Alzheimer's-like condition in dogs). Talk to your vet about these foods, which are primarily available through prescription and could make a real difference in your dog's symptoms.

Some foods also contain herbal supplements not officially approved for treating chronic conditions, but which may, anecdotally, offer relief from conditions like arthritis, itchy skin, digestive problems, and even depression. Use these foods with caution, however. If a food contains only trace amounts of a herb, it may have no effect whatsoever and you could be wasting your money.

If you are interested in trying supplements for your pet to address a particular problem, consider purchasing pet-specific supplements separately. Supplements prepared as supplements rather than as an additive to pet food are more likely to contain dosages appropriate to pets. Adding a herb to a pet food is a much more nebulous task. How do you know how much the dog will eat? Better to go with a separate supplement for the safest and most effective dosing. Talk to your holistic vet if you are interested in using herbal supplements.

Many dietary supplements legal for humans aren't yet technically legal for pets because they have no regulatory framework in which to exist. In the US, the National Animal Supplement Council (NASC) is currently working on building a place for animal supplements—many of which currently exist "under the radar" or as a "low-enforcement priority" in states unconcerned with substances that appear harmless. If and when they are successful, pet owners may find they have far more quality supplements available for their dogs.

Common Supplements for Dogs

- Probiotics for better digestion
- Glucosamine and chondroitin for healthy joints
- Omega-3 fatty acids from fish oil and/or flaxseed oil for healthy skin and coat
- Antioxidants for general immune health, energy, cognitive function, and possibly even as an anti-cancer agent

PROBLEMS AROUND FEEDING AND EATING

Most Goldens happily devour their meals then go about their

Sample Feeding Schedule for Each Phase of Your Golden's Life					
	PUPPIES (8 weeks to 6 months)	**ADOLESCENTS** (6 months to 1 year)	**ACTIVE ADULTS** (1 to 7 years)	**SEDENTARY ADULTS** (1 to 7 years)	**VETERANS** (7+ years)
Times per Day	3	2 to 3	2 to 3	2	2
Amount	The low end of recommended amount on food, or as much as the puppy will eat in ten minutes.	The low end of recommended amount on food, or slightly more if you can see his ribs. Or, as much as the adolescent will eat in ten minutes.	The low end to middle of amount on food, or slightly more on days of high activity. Or, as much as the dog will eat in ten minutes.	The low end of amount on food, or slightly less if dog is losing a noticeable waistline when viewed from above. Or, as much as the dog will eat in five minutes.	The low end of food, or slightly less if dog is losing a noticeable waistline or reducing activity level. Or, as much as the dog will eat in five minutes.
Best Food	Puppy food for large breeds specifically formulated to moderate growth, or a premium adult food.	Premium adult food.	Premium adult food for active dogs, or regular premium adult food.	Premium adult food.	Premium adult food or premium food designed for veterans.

merry way, but what if yours isn't among them? Every so often, a Golden Retriever will have an eating issue, but a few key strategies—and sometimes your vet—can help you solve these problems.

Digestive Upset

If your dog continually vomits or has diarrhoea after eating, try switching to a better food or a food with a different protein source (if your dog's food is chicken, try a food made with lamb, turkey, or fish). You can also try adding a spoonful of plain yogurt with active yogurt cultures to his food. If this doesn't help, call your vet. If your dog is losing weight even though he is eating, be sure to tell your vet right away. While digestive problems are usually a simple matter of a particular food disagreeing with your dog's system, there is a slight chance it could signal a more serious condition, so get it checked out.

Picky Eaters

So, your Golden thinks that dry food just isn't good enough unless it is soaked in meat juice and studded with tender chunks of all-white-meat chicken? Have you been feeding your dog too many table scraps? Sometimes, table scraps can result in a picky eater who won't eat without a little extra something special in the bowl. If this is the case, gradually reduce the amount of table food, then try adding a small spoonful of canned food each day. If your Golden gets hungry enough, he will eat it. Remember, Goldens are food motivated and will typically give in before too long. If your dog refuses to eat for more than 24 hours, give your vet a call. Call sooner than that if your dog shows any signs of discomfort like pacing, panting, abdominal tenderness, or swelling. Refusing to eat could signal a medical problem such as an intestinal obstruction or an episode of bloat, and these require immediate medical attention.

Food Obsession

If your Golden is so obsessed with food that you can't seem to get him to focus on anything else, it's time to broaden his horizons. Limit treats to healthy snacks like baby carrots and regular pieces of your dog's dry food. You might also increase the number of times you feed your Golden each day (remember also to reduce the amount of each meal accordingly), so your Golden feels more

A premium dog food should provide your Golden with all the nutrition he needs.

assured that food is usually coming soon. Also, consider whether you are promoting your dog's food obsession by focusing on food all the time in your interactions with your dog. Sure, it's good to have a pocket full of treats to keep your Golden focused on you, but if he is always more focused on your pocket than on you, it may be time to consider other alternatives.

You must teach your Golden that begging at the dinner table is not acceptable behaviour.

Food obsession can also result in some serious lapses in table manners. If your Golden is constantly begging, drooling, pawing your lap, or trying to steal food off the counters or the tables, he has the mistaken message that such behaviour is acceptable, or at least, that the consequences really aren't all that bad. How did he get that idea? Chances are, someone has been feeding him at the table, or at least dropping food on the floor. That tells your Golden that good things come from the family table and that he is likely to get some of them.

Time to nip this kind of behaviour in the bud. If your Golden can't behave while the family is eating, put him in his crate for some down time during the dinner hour. Or, put on his lead and collar and secure him near the table but not near enough to try to beg. Tell him to sit or lie down. The first time you try this, don't make him sit or lie down for very long—even one minute is enough. Then put him in his crate. You want him to be successful and earn his praise, and you want the time near the family to be a reward in itself. Increase the time in the sit or down every night until he is sitting politely throughout dinner, only rising at the end when the family rises to clear the table. If he behaves, he gets to hang out with the family the whole time! What a good dog!

And of course, if you want him to stop begging, never, ever, ever feed your Golden while sitting at the table. Goldens have good memories. If you do it once, they may always think there is hope that you will do it again. If you are giving your Golden healthy food leftovers, give them in your dog's bowl after dinner, as part of *his* dinner ritual, not *yours*.

Canine One-a-Day?

If you are feeding your dog a premium diet, you should have no need for multivitamin/mineral supplements. Your Golden's food should provide all the nutrition he needs.

Treat Issues

One of the reasons why Golden Retrievers are so easy to train is that they are so food motivated. If a dog will do anything for a treat, training is a breeze. If a dog doesn't like little pieces of turkey hotdogs, it can be a lot harder to convince him that sitting in a "down-stay" for five minutes is a really great idea.

But some people, including some trainers, don't like to train with "all treats all the time." Goldens are sensitive and responsive, so they respond much better to training methods that use positive reinforcement than those that use punishment. Fortunately, Goldens appreciate a lot of other rewards besides treats. Begin using other rewards during training, like praise and petting, a favourite toy, or a game of fetch. Sometimes, all your Golden really wants is a "Good dog!" and a nice stroke on the head from you. Alternate these rewards with treat rewards and you will keep your Golden guessing about what good things are coming next. That's more fun for everyone.

Treats can also be dangerous because people tend to give too many of them. A treat is just that…a treat. Something special, something anticipated—not something to be doled out every hour as a panacea for boredom. If treats are truly special, your Golden will be more motivated to try and get them by offering interesting behaviours which you can then reinforce in training.

Motivating With Food

While you do have to be careful not to overfeed your Golden, feed him at the table, or give him too many treats, you can use your Golden's naturally food-motivated nature for successful training. A tiny treat reward after a job well done keeps your Golden focused on you and what you might want him to do next. What a fun game—your Golden gets to work out what quirky thing you want him to do (sit, dance, roll over? Well, sure, why not!), and then you hand out the goodies.

Food can be an integral part of clicker training when you associate food with the neutral sound of a click. Food can become part of a post-walk or training session ritual. Even the daily meals

Does This Fur Make Me Look Fat?

Obesity is the most common health problem in pets today, and it can result in a host of problems throughout life, like low energy, arthritis, overworked internal organs, and fatigue. While your Golden may not look overweight to you, he may be fatter than you think. How can you tell?

First, stand over your Golden Retriever and look at him from the top. He should have a noticeable tuck-in at the waist. If his body looks like a sausage, he is overweight. Next, feel your dog's ribs. What ribs, you say? If you can't feel the ribs, your dog is overweight. You shouldn't be able to see ribs, but you should be able to feel them.

Because so many pets are overweight, a Golden Retriever at a healthy weight may look too thin to many pet owners. Take your vet's advice, however, if he or she tells you that your supposedly too-skinny Golden is just right. Monitor your Golden's weight frequently by looking for that waistline and feeling for those ribs. If you notice a weight gain, cut back on treats, slightly reduce portion size at meals, and add an extra ten minutes to that daily walk or vigorous game of fetch. Your Golden's weight problem is your problem, and you have the power to make it right.

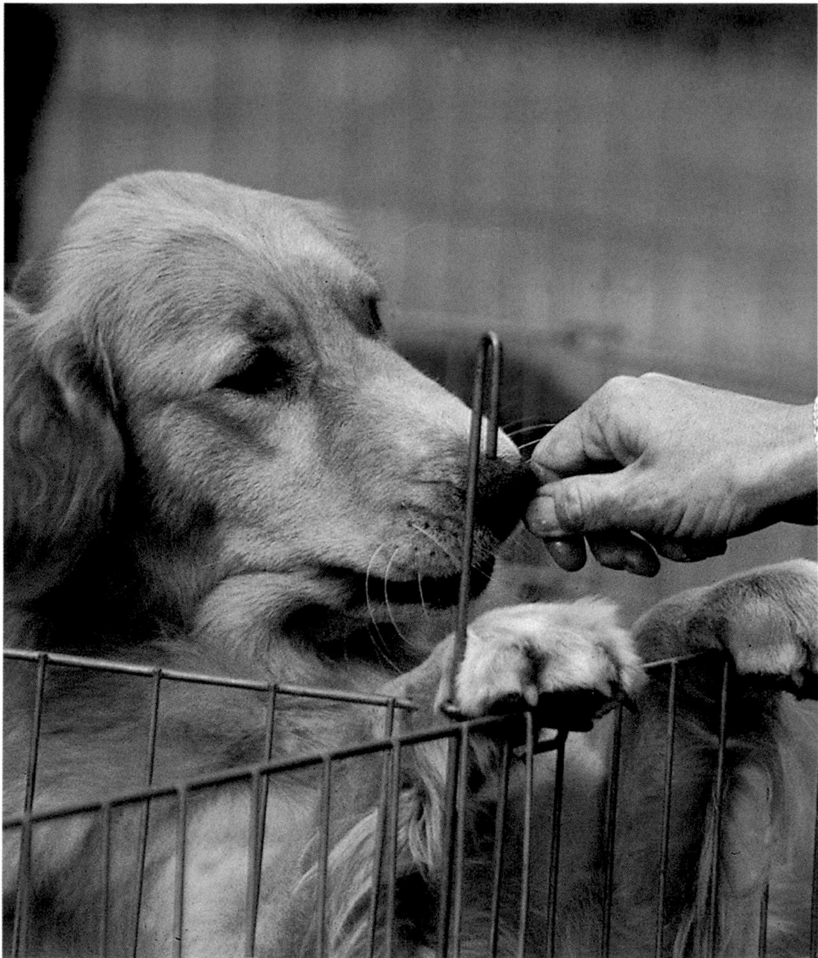

You can use your Golden's naturally food-motivated nature for successful training.

can be a motivator, if you always ask your Golden to execute a behaviour before you set down the food bowl. Many Goldens quickly learn to sit politely while their people put the food bowl down, not moving until they hear the "okay."

Food is not the enemy. It is your Golden's friend, and one important key to great health and a long, vibrant life. It is also a training tool, a concentrated pep talk, a gift, and a communication device. A treat tells your Golden, "You did a great job and I'm proud of you." And that's all your Golden really wants to hear.

Chapter 5

GROOMING
Your Golden Retriever

Grooming your Golden Retriever means keeping his beautiful, feathery golden coat tangle free and shiny. But it means more than that, too. Grooming isn't just about good looks, it is about good health, and a grooming routine is one of the most important things you can do to continually monitor your Golden's health.

Golden Retrievers are one of the easier breeds to groom. No hours of combing, no complicated stripping, or monthly baths necessary. The Golden coat has the beautiful silky flowing look of a long coat with the maintenance of a short coat—the best of both worlds. This chapter will show you how best to care for that coat, and how to integrate grooming into your Golden's daily routine…because good grooming is golden.

YOUR GOLDEN'S GROOMING ROUTINE

Your Golden Retriever doesn't need to be brushed and have his nails trimmed, or even have his teeth brushed every day. However, a daily grooming routine is a good idea, because a grooming check is also a daily health check. A daily grooming routine does more than alert you to any physical changes in your Golden Retriever. It also accustoms your Golden Retriever—particularly a Golden puppy—to the kind of handling your Golden will need to endure at the veterinary surgery.

A daily grooming routine is particularly important for Golden Retriever puppies. Daily grooming is an effective and gentle way to train your puppy to tolerate things like nail clipping and tooth brushing—things that an adult dog might have more difficulty accepting for the first time. Now is the time to teach your Golden Retriever some of the things necessary for life in a world with those strange humans who always seem to want to poke, prod, and palpitate, not to mention clip, trim, brush, and comb.

Choosing a Grooming Spot

Realistically, you can probably groom your Golden Retriever anywhere—on the couch, in the bathroom, on the patio. However, keep in mind that dogs feel comforted by routine, so if you always groom in the same spot at the same time, your Golden Retriever will know exactly what to expect when you take him to that special grooming spot.

Another consideration is what room to use if you are grooming indoors. Golden Retrievers shed, and because they have medium-length coats (some longer than others), that can translate to a lot of dog hair. While one good reason for brushing your Golden frequently is to collect dog hair in the brush so it doesn't get all over the house, you will still get some "fall-out" when brushing, so choose a place that is easy to clean. Tile floors can be swept, or choose a carpet that is easy to vacuum and a room without a lot of nooks and crannies or furniture that can hide tufts of Golden hair underneath.

If you are grooming indoors, some people have the space for a grooming table. Grooming tables are particularly convenient for small dogs and breeds that require long hours of brushing and combing. While it's not necessary for a breed like a Golden Retriever, if you have the space for a grooming table (maybe in a spare room or the basement) and you want to use one, you may find it easier to brush, trim, clip, and examine your Golden without having to bend over. Grooming tables are definitely more ergonomic.

Many people prefer to groom their Goldens outside. Goldens love to be outside with you, and if you have a convenient spot on the patio or porch for grooming, this can be an excellent option. Goldens tend to shed most prolifically in the autumn and spring when the weather is usually relatively mild, so if you groom inside most of the year, you might decide to groom outdoors during these seasons of heavier shedding.

Grooming for Better Bonding

You've heard it a hundred times: Golden Retrievers love to be with their people. You spend time with your Golden Retriever every day, walking, playing, or sitting on the couch watching television. But don't neglect the opportunity for human-dog bonding that the daily grooming routine provides.

When you groom your Golden Retriever, you are totally focused on him. You aren't doing anything else at the same time. Unlike other activities you and your Golden do together, grooming is all about you attending to your dog. What a great luxury for your Golden Retriever!

Goldens typically love grooming time, especially if you make it a positive and rewarding experience right from the beginning. Talk to your Golden while you brush his coat. Praise him when you check his eyes, ears, and feet. Gush over him when he sits nicely for nail trimming or lets you bathe him without leaping out of the tub and splattering water all over the house. This daily attention will go a long way towards building your relationship with your Golden and improving your communication. The more you pay attention to your Golden, the better you will understand each other, so make grooming a daily ritual and enjoy a closer relationship because of it.

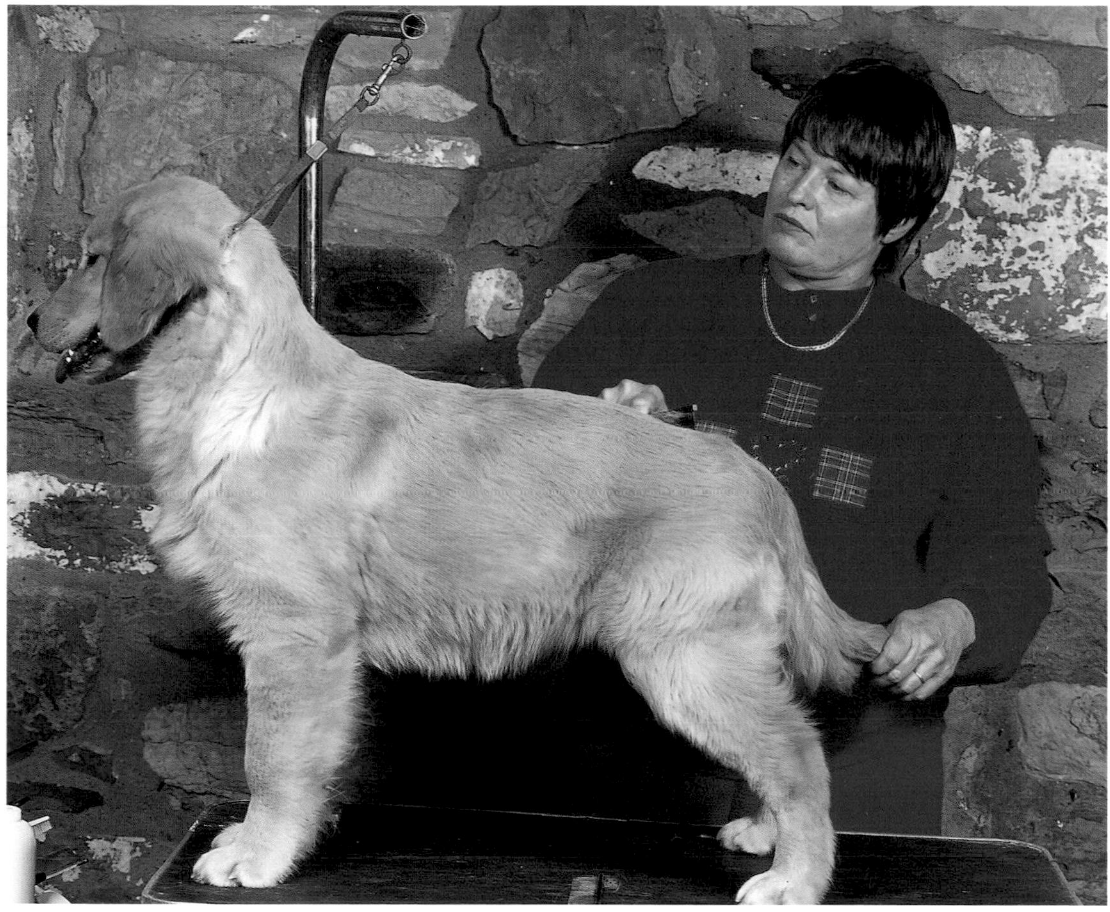

If you are grooming indoors, some people have the space for a grooming table.

Finally, consider where you will keep your grooming supplies. If you groom your Golden in the bathroom, can you designate space for a brush, comb, nail clippers, and Golden toiletries like shampoo and coat conditioner? If you groom outside, you might want to keep a basket of supplies somewhere near the door, so you can easily grab it and go.

Grooming Supplies

Once you have settled on a good spot for grooming, assemble your grooming supplies. While Golden Retrievers don't need too many grooming tools, a few key items and products will make grooming easy and convenient:

- Natural bristle brush. Your Golden's coat is one of his most beautiful attributes. Keep it that way with a natural bristle brush that won't tear your Golden's hair or irritate his skin.

- Coat rake. A coat rake will help loosen and pull out dead undercoat so your Golden stays mat free, especially during periods of heavy shedding.
- Steel comb. These combs get the tiniest tangles out of your Golden's coat. They can also comb out fleas, if necessary.
- Shampoo. Pet product manufacturers make hundreds of dog shampoos. Choose a basic shampoo, or one specially formulated for medium-length coats or for a Golden colour. If your Golden has sensitive skin, choose a shampoo designed to soothe the skin.
- Conditioner. Your Golden doesn't require a coat conditioner, but some people like to use them anyway to keep the coat smooth, shiny, and tangle free. Some conditioners made for dogs also have a nice aroma.
- Nail clippers. Choose clippers designed for large dogs, never nail clippers made for people. Some clippers come with a file or an electric smoother built into the clippers, to smooth out the rough nail surface after clipping. Or, you can use a nail grinder or even a dremel tool.
- Styptic pencil or powder to stop bleeding if you should accidentally clip the nail quick.
- Small blunt-tipped trimming scissors. Golden Retrievers tend to grow long hair between and around their paw pads. This can get tangled and in the winter, can collect balls of ice or irritating de-icing salt. Keep your Golden's paws trimmed, clipping out hair from between paw pads and around the feet.

Your Golden Daily Journal

You may not keep a diary, but keeping a daily (or even a weekly or monthly) record of your Golden Retriever's health condition, habits, and any changes you notice is more than just a nice way to look back on your Golden's early life. It can serve as an invaluable tool as your Golden ages, tracking the development of symptoms you might not even notice when they happen.

Your grooming journal can be a notebook or even a calendar. Just record the date, what you did (brush, clip nails, apply pest control, etc.), and anything in particular you notice, such as your Golden's appetite or lack of it that day, whether he was drinking more than the usual amount of water, any skin changes, behavior changes, or anything else you think seems worth recording. If you get in the habit of writing down anything related to your Golden's grooming, diet, health, and behaviour, you will be able to look back and work out exactly when certain symptoms started to happen, when you started giving your Golden a particular medication, or when you first noticed that sensitive spot or limp or bare patch.

Your vet will also appreciate this written record when she asks questions like "When did you first notice a decrease in appetite?" or "How long has your Golden had this lump?"

Brushing your Golden Retriever is the easiest way to keep his coat clean and shiny.

- Ear wash and cotton-wool balls. Some products have pads presoaked in ear wash, for easy use.
- Toothbrush and toothpaste made for dogs.
- Pest control product. If you live in a flea-prone area, ask your vet about a monthly spot-on product to keep fleas and ticks away.
- Washcloth for wiping face and eyes.
- Petroleum jelly, to keep eyes protected during baths.
- Soft scrub brush, for bathing.
- A large cup or pitcher for rinsing the coat during a bath, if you don't have a handheld showerhead.
- A large fluffy bath towel for towel-drying your Golden's coat.
- A hair-dryer with a cool setting (optional).

1-2-3 GROOM

You've got your spot, you've got your tools and products. Now you are ready to start grooming! Grooming entails certain daily steps, certain weekly steps, and certain monthly steps, as well as seasonal concerns. Remember, your Golden responds best to routine, so try to follow a schedule that works for you. (See the box at the end of this chapter for a typical grooming routine for your Golden.) Choose a set time to groom every day—or even every other day, every third day, or once a week. (Daily is ideal, but weekly is much better than randomly, or not at all!) Grooming sessions can be tailored to your individual preference and your Golden's tendencies, but in general, try to include the following steps.

Seasonal Shedding

Many breeds shed all year long, but most breeds, including Golden Retrievers, experience heavier periods of shedding in the spring and autumn. Golden Retrievers have a double coat—a long, silky outer coat and a downy, insulating undercoat. In the spring, much of this undercoat sheds out and can get caught in the outer coat, forming mats, particularly around the ears, tail, and "underarm," where the front legs meet the chest. In the autumn, the undercoat grows in more thickly again. During both these periods, Goldens need extra grooming with a natural bristle brush and an undercoat rake to prevent mats and keep their coats looking clean, bright, and shiny.

Brushing

Brushing your Golden Retriever is the easiest way to keep his coat clean and shiny, and to keep your home free of big golden tufts of fur. Brushing distributes the natural coat oils to the ends of the hair. It stimulates skin circulation, and pulls the dull, dead hairs out of the coat. You don't really need to brush your Golden Retriever every day, but if you do, you will probably need to vacuum less often. Plus, brushing is a great way to bond with your dog. Most Golden Retrievers love the feeling of being brushed, and love the fact that you are spending some focused time on them.

When brushing your Golden Retriever, be sure to groom the entire coat. Here is one method to get the most out of brushing:

- First, brush the body coat in the opposite direction of growth, from tail towards the head.
- Next, brush in the direction of growth, from head to tail.
- Brush your Golden's head and ears carefully, or use a steel comb for these areas.
- Brush down each leg, paying special attention to the mat-prone areas where the legs meet the body.
- Brush your Golden's chest and belly.
- Brush the tail, paying special attention to the mat-prone area at the base of the tail.
- Once a week, follow brushing with a thorough combing. Use a steel comb and be sure to comb from the skin, to catch any mats or tangles close to the coat that you might not see or feel with a brush. This is a good time to check for signs of fleas.

Get your Golden puppy accustomed to regular baths at a young age.

- During periods of heavy shedding, use the coat rake to pull out the dead undercoat more efficiently.

Bathing

If your Golden spends most of his time indoors, he probably won't need baths very often. Unlike some breeds, Goldens don't have scent glands that give them that musky dog smell. A healthy, well-brushed coat actually sheds dirt efficiently, so after a romp in a dirty pond, your Golden can drip dry, shake a few times, and the dirt will fall off.

After his bath, towel dry your Golden's coat as well as you can.

However, a monthly bath will keep your Golden clean and smelling nice, and can keep parasites and bacteria at bay on dogs that spend a lot of time outside. You might also need to bathe your Golden if he gets into dirty water, rolls in a dead animal, or plays in the mud.

Bathing a Golden is relatively easy because Goldens like water. However, they might not like standing in the bathtub, so get your Golden puppy accustomed to regular baths at a young age, when your Golden is physically easier to control. Also, make sure you wear something that can get wet. It is almost impossible to bathe a dog as large as a Golden and not get a little bit wet. Even if you get through most of the bath relatively unscathed, your Golden will probably shake to get the water out of his coat at the end, so be prepared.

In the warm weather, you might want to bathe your Golden Retriever outside, using the hose. A child's small plastic swimming pool works well for this purpose, and your Golden will probably think the whole affair is a big game. Washing your dog in your bathing suit outside on a warm summer day can be fun for you, too. Or, this could be a good project for older kids.

If bathing your Golden outdoors, reward him afterwards with a fun game of "catch the hose water" or Frisbee. Avoid "roll in the mud puddle," however, or you'll have to start all over again! After an indoor bath, offer a treat or a game of fetch for a job well done. If you don't want your Golden to get dirty again, keep him inside until he is dry.

Here are the steps to follow, to make bath time as easy as possible for everyone:

- Assemble everything you need before your Golden is in the tub, wet, and ready to jump out and run around the house when you realise you forgot to grab the shampoo. Here is what you need: shampoo, conditioner (optional), scrub brush, petroleum jelly (optional), and a large cup or jug for rinsing, if you don't have a hand-held sprayer.
- Brush your Golden Retriever thoroughly before getting the coat wet. Wet tangles tend to get tighter, so be sure the coat is tangle free.
- If you think you might get soap in your Golden's eyes, put a dab of petroleum jelly at the corner of each eye, to repel soap and water.
- Run the bathwater or turn on the hose. Check the temperature. It should be lukewarm to cool. If you are bathing your Golden outside, be sure you run the hose long enough to run out all the water that has been sitting there. That water can get scalding hot!
- Get your Golden in the tub! This can be tricky if your Golden doesn't like the idea. Use a treat and lure the dog in the tub or swimming pool. Have a toy handy for distraction and chewing. If your Golden doesn't want to stay put, use his collar and clip on a lead. Hold on to this or clip it to something sturdy, at least until your Golden has had enough baths that he learns to stand nicely and stay for his bath.

Bathing Tip

Brush your dog's fur before you get it wet.

One of the most important things you can do to prevent nail trimming from being an unpleasant experience is to make it rewarding to your puppy.

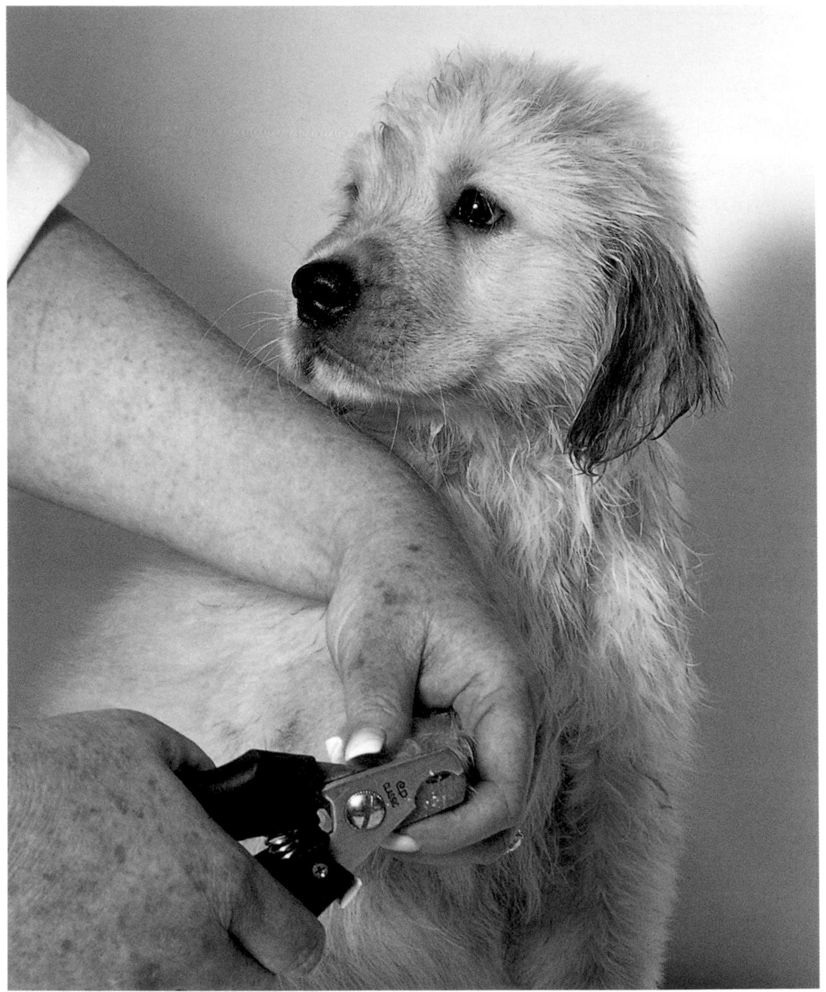

- Get your Golden's coat wet, all the way down to the skin, so the undercoat gets wet, too.
- Using your hands or a soft brush, work shampoo into your Golden's coat, all the way down to the skin. Massage the skin to work the shampoo into a lather. Don't forget the belly, legs, and under the tail.
- Using a handheld sprayer, the hose, or a large cup or jug, rinse the coat thoroughly. This might take longer than you think because of your Golden's double coat. Go over the coat several times, working out soap with your hands or the brush, until the water runs clear and you see no more evidence of soap. If you leave soap in the coat, it will encourage tangles and irritate the skin.

- If you are using coat conditioner, apply this to the coat and rinse. (Or, if the coat conditioner is for spraying on after the bath, do as directed.)
- Towel dry your Golden's coat as well as you can. Your Golden will likely help you out with a few good shakes.
- Your Golden's coat can certainly air-dry, but you can speed the process with a hair-dryer set to the low or cool setting. When blow-drying your Golden, keep the dryer at least 6 inches away from the coat to prevent burning. Brush while blow-drying. Some Goldens really enjoy the warm dryer and the extra pampering, once they get used to the strange sound of that noisy machine.

Nail Trimming

Nail trimming is important—if your Golden's nails get too long, he could inadvertently scratch people, and long nails that cause the foot pads to splay could actually damage your Golden's feet. Nails should be short, neat, and smooth, and the best way to accomplish this is to trim your Golden's nails a little bit every week, rather than a lot every couple of months.

Inside every dog's nail is a little vein called the quick. The longer the nail grows, the further down the nail the quick grows. When you clip your Golden's nails, you have to be careful not to clip the quick. This is painful to your Golden, and can make him fear nail clipping. It also causes bleeding which can be difficult to stop. To be safe, have a styptic pencil or other product made to stop bleeding. The bleeding will stop eventually, but in the meantime, you risk getting blood all over the house.

Baby Steps

If you have neglected nail trimming for awhile and your Golden's nails are long, don't try to cut them down all at once. Trim off just a little, every day or two, until they are down to size. This will allow the quick to recede back from the nail and you will be less likely to clip it by mistake.

Start nail trimming right away so your Golden gets used to it. Puppies may not like it, but they will get used to it if you do it regularly. A large adult dog that hasn't been trained to do this may put up quite a struggle.

One of the most important things you can do to prevent nail trimming from being an unpleasant experience is to make it rewarding to your puppy. At first, just do one nail each day, trimming daily instead of weekly. This will get your Golden puppy used to the routine. Work up to one paw each day. Take it slowly, and offer lots of praise, rewards, and a fun play session afterwards. The goal is to get your Golden to look forward to nail trimming, because he knows what great things will result. Eventually, work

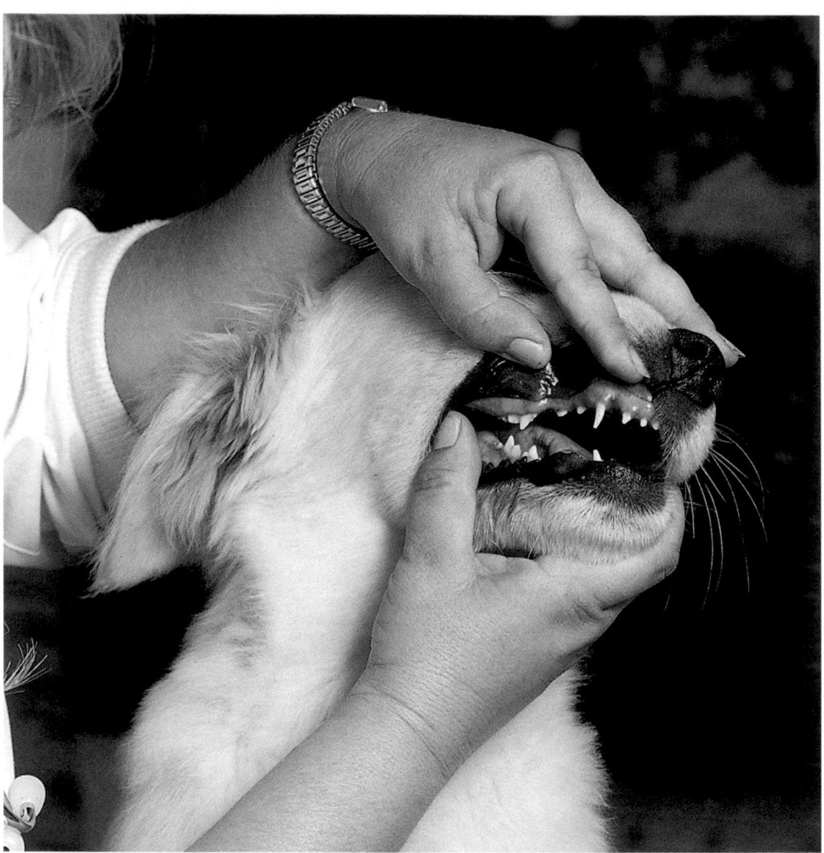

Dental care is an essential part of your Golden's grooming routine.

up to doing all the nails on all the paws once a week. For puppies who really don't like nail trimming, keep the sessions very short and positive. Be patient and persistent—your Golden will learn to accept it. Remember how important nail trimming is!

To make nail trimming as easy and relaxed as possible, follow these steps:

- Collect nail clippers, styptic pencil, and treats or a favourite toy. Call your Golden. Praise and reward him when he comes, rather than immediately bringing out the nail clippers. You don't want your Golden to associate "come" with something unpleasant!
- Pick up your Golden's paw. If you have been handling his paws every day in your grooming sessions, this should be effortless.
- Take the nail clippers and position them around the nail. Clip off just the tip quickly, to make a clean cut.
- Do the rest of the nails on that paw.
- File the end of each nail with a file or grinder so it is smooth.
- Repeat with the other paws.

Your Golden's Grooming Schedule

The Daily Groom

Here are suggested steps to take during your daily grooming session:

1. First, call your Golden to you and praise and pet him. Take him to the grooming spot.
2. Rub your Golden's coat all over with your hands, massaging his skin and loosening dead hair with your fingers. Feel for any lumps, bumps, rashes, or skin changes. Pay attention to the condition of your dog's coat. Is it silky and shiny or dry and dull? Also, pay attention to any sore spots, if your Golden flinches or yelps while you do this. If you notice anything unusual, give your vet a call.
3. Check inside your Golden's ears, check his eyes and nose for discharge, and check under his tail. Make sure everything looks clean and healthy. If you notice anything unusual, give your vet a call.
4. Brush your Golden all over with the natural bristle brush. Don't forget the tail!
5. Wipe down your Golden's face, eyes, and inside ear leather with a warm, moist washcloth or cotton-wool balls.
6. Pick up each foot and look at the paw pads, nails, and hair.
7. Brush your Golden's teeth using a brush and paste made for dogs. Check for any sore spots, missing teeth, or tartar buildup.
8. Record what you did and anything you noticed in your dog's daily journal.

The Weekly Groom

Once a week, add these steps to your Golden's grooming routine:

1. Check for any long paw pad hair and trim feet with scissors.
2. Check nails and clip off just the tips, to keep them nice and short and to keep the quick retracted.
3. After brushing, comb through the coat, all the way down to the skin, paying special attention to mat-prone areas like behind the ears, under the tail, and under the "arms."
4. Check for signs of fleas: black specks or the tiny jumping insects themselves.
5. Wash out ears with ear wash and dry them.

The Monthly Groom

Once a month, add these steps to your Golden's grooming routine:

1. Give your Golden a bath.
2. Apply pest control spot-on, if necessary.

The Seasonal Groom

During shedding season, brush with the coat rake to remove shedding undercoat. You may need to do this daily for a few weeks during heavy shedding seasons.

Moisture can get trapped in the ears of floppy-eared breeds, creating yeast infections.

Ear Care

Because Golden Retrievers have floppy ears, they can be prone to yeast infections when moisture gets trapped inside, creating a breeding ground for yeast. Yeast infections are itchy and unpleasant for your Golden and require medication from the vet. Ears can also be afflicted with ear mites and can get dirt and bacteria inside, especially if your Golden spends a lot of time outside in the undergrowth or swimming in natural bodies of water.

If you notice your Golden scratching his ears a lot, give your vet a call. The best way to prevent infection from occurring in the first place, however, is to keep your Golden's ears clean and dry. Here's how:

- Assemble your supplies: cotton-wool balls, cotton buds, and a commercial ear wash or a vinegar-water solution at a proportion of 1:1.
- Wet a cotton-wool ball with the ear wash or vinegar-water and wipe out your Golden's ear, under the ear leather and around the inside of the ear, as far as you can see.
- Wet a cotton bud with the ear wash or vinegar-water and use it to clean all the little creases, nooks, and crannies. *Do not stick the cotton bud down into the ear canal past where you can see.*
- Dry your Golden's ears with a dry cotton ball, removing as much moisture as you can.
- If you see any ear mites (tiny bugs) or if the inside of your Golden's ear looks red or irritated, give your vet a call. Treating ear infections usually requires medication from the vet.

Eye Care

Some breeds tend to have a lot of eye problems like runny eyes or dry eyes, but Golden Retrievers usually don't suffer from these problems. However, wiping your dog's eyes with a moist cloth each day can keep them clean and bright. Check your Golden's eyes at least weekly for signs of discharge, redness, irritation, or debris. Allergies, debris, or a condition called entropion that causes the eyelid to turn inward, irritating the cornea, can all cause eye irritation. Also check for signs of cloudiness, which could signal cataracts, a rare condition that can sometimes occur in Golden Retrievers at any age.

Dental Care

Dental care is not only an essential part of your Golden's

grooming routine, it could save his life! An elderly dog with teeth covered in plaque can be at a greater risk for early death and heart disease. Studies show that in dogs (and in humans!), dental plaque can lead to bacterial infections of the heart, so keeping your Golden's teeth clean from the start is important. Daily brushing can prevent the need for professional teeth cleaning later in life, an expensive procedure that requires anaesthesia. They say prevention is the best medicine, and this is certainly true when it comes to your Golden's dental health. Just as with nail clipping and brushing, puppies that learn to accept tooth brushing at a young age will happily accept the process as adults, especially if you always make it rewarding with lots of praise and a fun game of fetch afterwards. Here's what you'll need to know for good doggy dental care:

- Toothpaste. Always use a toothpaste made for dogs. Toothpastes made for humans can upset your dog's stomach.

Care and attention to grooming will leave your Golden looking and feeling great.

- Toothbrush. Use a long-handled toothbrush made for dogs. If your Golden really dislikes the toothbrush, you can wipe his teeth with a cloth, or buy one of the toothbrushes that fits over your finger.
- To get your Golden used to the process, let him lick some toothpaste off your finger for a few days in a row. Also, practise brushing without the paste, to get him used to letting you pull up his lips and rub his teeth.
- Be sure to get the front, back, and surface of all the teeth and concentrate on the gumline, where plaque tends to accumulate. An added benefit: a clean mouth doesn't harbor bacteria and can cure bad doggy breath!

Bad Breath

If you're taking care of your dog's teeth every day and he still has bad breath, see your vet.

Bad Breath Beaters

You love it when your Golden gives you kisses, but certainly you don't love that bad doggy breath! Dogs should not have foul breath, and if they do, there could be a serious cause, including gum disease or a mouth infection, or even a foreign body stuck somewhere in your dog's mouth, such as a bone, some dirt, or rotten food.

Most of the time, however, your dog's mouth just needs a good cleaning. Daily brushing with a toothbrush and dog toothpaste will usually resolve halitosis in your Golden Retriever. Many companies make dog treats designed to curb bad breath, but fresh raw vegetables and fruits that are crunchy can help clean teeth and freshen breath, too. Try raw baby carrots or chunks of raw apples. These are better for your Golden than processed dog biscuits, which often contain excess calories, preservatives, and even sugar. Raw vegetables are also good sources of vitamins and fibre. (Never give your dog raw onions or grapes, however. These are toxic to dogs, and wouldn't improve his breath anyway!)

If you are brushing your Golden's teeth every day and he still has foul breath, see your vet to rule out serious problems. If something is stuck somewhere in your dog's mouth or throat, your vet can find it and remove it safely. In rare cases, bad breath could even signal an oral tumour or lung cancer, so have your vet check out bad breath you just can't resolve. Your vet can also prescribe a special mouth spray or even a prescription food to improve the problem.

PROFESSIONAL GROOMERS

Golden Retrievers may have silky, flowing fur but they don't usually require professional grooming. No trimming, stripping, shaping, or primping required! However, some people like to take their dogs to the groomers for the occasional bath and nail clipping. Professional groomers do the work for you—for a fee.

Groomers come in many guises. Some groomers will groom while you wait. Others expect you to drop off your dog and pick him up later. Still others, called mobile groomers, have vans or motor homes equipped for grooming. They park in your driveway and groom your dog right there on your property. Mobile groomers may cost a little more, but are convenient and save your Golden Retriever from having to sit in a kennel waiting for you to pick him up.

Some vets employ groomers, and so do some pet stores, especially some of the larger chains. Some provide you with shopping opportunities and even coffee shops, so you can stay nearby as your dog is groomed. Some groomers simply groom in their own homes, as a home-based business. This booming profession keeps expanding and most towns have at least one dog groomer—but do a little research before you drop off your Golden Retriever for grooming; it's important to check out your options and choose the right groomer for you.

If you choose to use a professional groomer, here are a few things to look for:

- Groomers should have some professional training, and preferably will have certification or other proof of training posted at their grooming establishment.
- The establishment should be clean, neat, and well organised.
- The groomer should be professional and not appear too hurried or overwhelmed. You want to be sure you are leaving your Golden in good hands!
- Be sure you and the groomer agree beforehand on exactly what services you want, and how much they will cost. Prices should be posted.
- Get recommendations. If your friends all rave about this or that groomer, that's a good sign. Ask around and don't leave your precious pup with just anyone.
- Shop around. Price and quality may vary quite a bit from groomer to groomer, but keep in mind price doesn't necessarily indicate quality. Again, ask around.

Chapter 6

TRAINING AND BEHAVIOUR of Your Golden Retriever

Some people have the curious idea that Golden Retrievers don't need training, that by their very natures, they are practically pretrained and perfectly well behaved. Dog obedience instructors love seeing Golden Retrievers in their basic obedience classes. Why? They know this is a breed that is easy to train. So, why does your Golden Retriever seem the furthest thing from the ideal obedience pupil, especially during puppyhood or the ultra-active adolescent period? Will your Golden Retriever ever settle down and listen to you? Can you ever get him to hold a "down-stay" for more than a few seconds? Will he someday stop dragging you down the street by the lead?

Training a Golden Retriever really is easy, especially compared to training many other breeds less oriented towards working closely with humans. But Golden Retrievers certainly don't come pre-trained to act like little golden angels, and the simple fact is that any dog, and particularly any retriever, will behave in certain ways that humans just don't like. They chew. They dig. They bark. They try to score the roast chicken on the counter. And then they chew some more.

However, the good news is that early training and socialisation, regular practice sessions, and consistency make the job much easier. That means you have some work to do before your Golden Retriever will be the envy of the neighbourhood for his good citizenship. Here's what you need to know.

SOCIALISATION

Socialisation is the process of introducing dogs to the human world. We have a lot of things going on that dogs don't necessarily understand, yet we expect them to deal with these things without acting too much like dogs. We don't want them to bite, growl, snarl, bark too much, or quiver in fear when they encounter new people, other animals, or strange situations. But dogs have natural instincts to do some of these things when confronted with the unfamiliar. They are simply protecting themselves. They are being dogs.

Socialisation helps dogs understand that most of the time, they don't need to protect themselves, and can trust humans to protect them. This is also natural, in a way, for dogs. Dogs look to a leader to follow, so they don't have to endure the constant stress of independent survival. Socialisation reinforces to dogs that humans are generally friendly, well-meaning creatures and the source of yummy treats, kind words, gentle stroking, and protection. It also schools dogs in some of the finer points of living with humans. For instance, socialisation can help dogs to understand that children are just shorter, faster-moving humans, great for playing but not for chewing on or knocking over. It teaches dogs that humans come in many different sizes, colours, and shapes, and with a variety of accessories, from bicycles and scooters to wheelchairs, walking

The best way to socialise your naturally friendly Golden is to expose him to many different kinds of people, situations, and other pets at a young age.

Good Ways to Socialise Your Golden Retriever

- Take your puppy to puppy socialisation classes. This is a great opportunity to meet many different people and other dogs under controlled conditions and the practiced guidance of an instructor, who can also answer questions and give you other socialisation ideas.
- Have a puppy party. Invite friends over and have them gently play with your puppy and offer him treats. One at a time, please! No need to overwhelm a young puppy. Keep it fun.
- Take your Golden Retriever on a walk through the neighbourhood at least once per day. Vary your route so you come into contact with different people and places.
- Golden Retrievers who learn to travel in the car at a young age think car trips are just great! Unless, of course, the only place they ever go is to the vet. Take your Golden Retriever in the car often to parks, on hikes, on picnics, to football games, or wherever dogs are allowed. However, never ever leave a Golden Retriever alone in a car in warm weather. Cars heat up very quickly, even when you don't think it is hot outside, and many dogs die each year from heat stroke associated with being left inside a car.

sticks, and walkers, and that none of these things require a fearful or aggressive response. It also teaches dogs that they can live with or at least pass by other animals without feeling the need to chase them, jump on them, play with them uninvited, or attack them.

Because dogs are naturally social creatures, they take to socialisation well, in most cases. Without it, however, dogs may grow up fearful, agitated, suspicious, or even aggressive, and will often respond to situations in a way that is unacceptable to humans. Many dogs are abandoned to rescue centres each year, simply because they have never been taught how to fit into the human world.

The best way to socialise your naturally friendly and sociable Golden Retriever is to expose him to many different kinds of people, situations, and other pets at a young age. While puppies should not be put at risk for disease and should probably avoid crowded dog parks full of many different dogs before they are fully vaccinated, you can still take your puppy with you to many different places, you can invite friends over frequently to meet and play with your puppy, and you can go on walks around the neighbourhood to meet the neighbours, the neighbouring pets, and to learn about cars, bicycles, and all the other things that whiz, trot, scamper, or dash by in cities, suburbs, small towns, or even out in the country.

One important thing to remember about socialisation, however: these early interactions must all be positive! A frightening tangle with a large dog, an aggressive human, a rowdy child, or a loud noise can make a permanent impression on a young puppy, having the opposite effect of what you intend. You are your Golden Retriever's guardian, so teach him about the wide, wide world, but at the same time, make sure he knows that you will protect him and keep him safe. If your dog trusts that the people you know and the places you go are sure to be safe, fun, and rewarding, then he will grow up to be a happy, self-confident, friendly dog with a good instinct about people and situations. That, of course, is what we all want in a companion animal.

CRATE TRAINING

Crate training is one of the most important things you can do for your new Golden Retriever. Crate training serves many purposes. It gives your Golden Retriever a private, quiet place to go when he needs some downtime. It gives you a way to control an exuberant dog when you don't have time to enact other training strategies. It helps your Golden have better habits, and contributes to a regular schedule. And, perhaps most importantly, it is an invaluable tool in housetraining your Golden Retriever.

Crate training is simply the process of getting your Golden Retriever used to his crate. This isn't difficult because dogs are natural den animals, and they feel safer when they have an enclosed

Always introduce two dogs while on a lead and under control.

Dogs want and need the security of a den, and a crate is a den custom made for dogs.

area for sleeping or resting. In a crate, the dog only has to pay attention to one opening, in front of him. The sides and back are secure, so the dog can relax and not have to worry about anybody sneaking up on him. Instinctually, this is less stressful for dogs.

People who don't give their Golden Retrievers a crate often comment that their dogs seek out crate-like spaces. They might try to sleep under your desk while you are working, or rest under a dining room chair. Dogs want and need the security of a den, and a crate is a den custom made for dogs.

Choosing a Crate

When choosing a crate, look for one that has solid sides or, if wire-sided, can easily be covered with a blanket. If your dog can see on all sides, that defeats the purpose of feeling secure. A crate should be large enough for your Golden to stand up, turn around, and lie down in comfortably, but not so large that he could use one side as a bathroom and the other side as a bedroom. For a small puppy, put a box or other barrier in the crate to artificially reduce the size, until your puppy is large enough to use the whole space. That way, you won't have to buy one crate for the puppy and another for the adult-sized dog. Some crates can even buckle into a seatbelt in the car for safe travel, a feature you might consider.

Using a Crate

When you first bring home your Golden Retriever, your goal is to make the first interactions with the crate positive. Put the crate where you plan to keep it, keeping in mind that until your Golden Retriever is housetrained, he will probably sleep there at night, and that dogs like to know where you are. If not within view of your bed, it should at least be in a warm, comfortable place nearby, within hearing range of you.

Put a soft blanket, fleece, pillow, or other soft covering inside the crate, then tuck a few treats inside, too. A tennis ball or other toy will make the inside of the crate even more appealing. Then, bring your Golden Retriever into the room. Let him explore. If he smells the treats, he might go right in, and may come right out. Different dogs react to the crate in different ways. Some might settle right into the soft blanket and have a nice time eating the treat. Others might be nervous about going in for the first time. Don't try to force him inside the crate. Let him take his time, but if he does go in, praise him and give him another treat or a toy. You might also show him a treat, then toss it in the crate. Many puppies will go in to get the treat.

Even if your Golden Retriever comes right back out, that's fine. He will get used to the crate in his own time. After you Golden Retriever has had a chance to relieve himself outside and has explored your home and the crate for a while, lead him into his crate or gently put him in with a treat and a toy, and close the door. Some dogs don't mind at all. Others might whimper or cry. Don't make a big deal about this, but you can say a few cheerful,

Until your puppy is well trained, go outside with him for "toilet breaks."

encouraging words to your Golden Retriever. Stay within view for a while, then leave the room for short periods, but keep coming back, to reinforce that you are nearby. When you are out of the room, say something occasionally so your Golden Retriever can hear you.

The first night, or first few nights, in the crate can be trying for everyone. Just remember that your new dog is adjusting to a whole new environment, and that can be stressful and a little scary. New human babies cry a lot, too, but luckily, Golden Retriever puppies adjust and mature much faster than human babies! Just keep reassuring your Golden Retriever without getting too emotional about it, which will only increase his stress.

Goldens and Other Pets

Golden Retrievers don't tend to be aggressive towards other dogs, but always introduce two dogs while on a lead and under control. Let them sniff each other and make their acquaintance, but keep control until you know both dogs plan to get along. Golden Retrievers may tend to chase cats and other small animals, but those exposed to the family cat from the beginning are usually just fine. Let the cat and dog get to know each other, but keep the puppy from jumping all over the cat. Not only will the cat probably dislike this kind of attention, but many puppies have been seriously injured by cat scratches. Your Golden Retriever does not need to learn how to play with the pet rodents or birds. Protect all your pets!

During the day, use the crate whenever you can't directly supervise your Golden Retriever, until he is reliably and completely housetrained. Pretty soon, your Golden Retriever will probably go in there on his own, just because he likes his soft, comfy, treat-filled little spot. That's when you know you have achieved crate training success.

Some helpful tips for easier crate training:

- Always put a treat or two and a toy or two in the crate, so your Golden Retriever associates the crate with yummy rewards and favourite things.
- Never leave a young puppy in a crate for more than two or three hours. An adult dog should not be left in the crate for more than four hours, except at night-time.
- Never use the crate as punishment. It can be a calming, time-out space but you should never throw the dog in the crate in anger.
- During the day, after your Golden is housetrained, keep the crate door open so your Golden Retriever can go in and out whenever he chooses.
- Bring the crate with you when you travel with your dog, so he always has a familiar place to go, no matter where you are. This will help to relieve any stress associated with travel.
- Use the crate in the car or van, if possible, to keep your Golden Retriever safe (or use a dog seatbelt).
- In rare cases, individual dogs may truly dislike their crates and may not adjust to one. If so, housetrain your Golden using the schedule training method, described below, and find an alternative method for keeping your Golden safe and secure when you are away, such as a puppy-proofed room, enclosed with a door or tall baby gate, filled with lots of Nylabones or other acceptable things to chew.

HOUSETRAINING

The first training priority for most new dog owners is housetraining. This is definitely job number one for any dog living with humans! Fortunately, Golden Retrievers are one of the easiest breeds to housetrain, especially if you combine two highly effective methods: crate training and schedule training.

Puppies don't come to you understanding that you care one way or another where they relieve themselves. But obviously you do care, so the whole point of housetraining is to communicate to your Golden Retriever where and when you would prefer that

Sample Housetraining Schedule

This may look like a lot of trips to the garden at first, but remember that the older your Golden Retriever gets, the less often he will have to go "out." Take young puppies out to the special spot in the garden any time they begin to sniff and circle, and also:

- First thing in the morning
- 15 minutes after breakfast
- Right after midmorning nap
- 15 minutes after lunch
- Right after midafternoon nap or play session
- 15 minutes after dinner
- Right before bed
- At least once in the middle of the night, when they wake up

As your puppy gets older and more controlled, you can cut down this schedule like this:

- First thing in the morning
- After breakfast
- At midday
- After dinner
- Right before bed

Dogs are creatures of habit, and a consistent, rigorous schedule like this will teach your Golden Retriever exactly what that trip out into the garden is for.

he "do his business." Your Golden Retriever doesn't want to do things to make you angry or stain your carpet, but when a dog has to go, a dog has to go. Therefore, the key to this process is to reward your dog when he does what you want, and to keep him from ever making a mistake.

Supervision is very important in this process. Young puppies do certain things when they are getting ready to relieve themselves. Typically, they begin to sniff the ground a lot while moving constantly, sometimes in circles, looking for a good spot. If you learn to recognise this behaviour, you can quickly whisk your puppy outside to the spot where you want him to go, then praise him when he relieves himself outside.

Also, remember that puppies (and adult dogs) would rather be with you than alone. Many a pet owner has wondered why the puppy waits and waits at the back door, then relieves himself as soon as he comes inside. Of course he does! He wants the exciting events of his day to happen near the people he loves.

Until your puppy is well trained, go outside with him. This not only keeps him company, but allows you to praise him immediately when he relieves himself in the right spot. This will

The Importance of Training

According to a recent Americacn study conducted by the National Council on Pet Population Study and Policy (NCPPSP) 96 percent of dogs relinquished to rescue centres have had no obedience training. Chances are, if these dogs had been better trained, their behaviour would have been more manageable and they would never have lost their homes. Obedience training your dog can truly make the difference between a pet you can't handle and a lifelong companion.

be even more effective if you take him out on his lead each time, to the spot you want him to use. Be patient. It may take a while, but don't let him off the lead until he "goes." This is his reward for a job well done. Praise him, unclip the lead, and let him romp around for a bit, maybe even chase and retrieve a tennis ball. This makes the whole process fun and exciting for your puppy. Why would he want to relieve himself inside if doing so outside is so much fun and gets such an enthusiastic reaction from you?

When Mistakes Happen

Housetraining errors are usually human errors. It is your job to know when your Golden Retriever needs to relieve himself, and to give him the opportunity to do so in the right place. If you make a mistake, miss a cue, stop watching, or don't take your puppy out on schedule, don't punish him for your mistake! If you can whisk him outside while he is going, do so. Don't yell, hit, or make a big deal out of it, but praise when he finishes outside. If you just find the puddle or pile, say nothing. Clean it up so no smell remains (dogs tend to go where they smell that they have gone before), but don't scold your puppy. Unless you catch him in the act, he won't know what you are scolding him about. And for heaven's sake, don't rub his nose in his mess! This doesn't make sense to him. He'll only think that you are scary and unpredictable, and possibly that when he relieves himself in the house, he better do it in a spot that you won't find. This is not the message you want to send. Just consider this a missed opportunity, and say nothing. But the next time he gets it right, remember to tell him what a good job he did!

But you and your puppy don't have to make housetraining mistakes. The trick is to maintain vigilant supervision, and to take your puppy outside when he needs to go. This is where crate training and schedule training come into play.

Crate Training

Crate training works on the principle that dogs do not like to soil where they sleep. If the crate gives your Golden Retriever just enough space to sleep comfortably, he probably will not want to use the crate as a toilet. That means that when you cannot directly supervise your Golden Retriever, you can keep him in his crate, knowing that he will instinctually control himself when in the crate—as long as you don't leave him in there longer than his little puppy bladder can handle! If you leave a puppy in a crate for more than a couple of hours at a time, you are setting him up for failure. If you take him out often, you will give him the opportunity to get it right. That's the goal. If you take him out on a regular schedule, you'll have even better success.

Schedule Training

Schedule training works on the principle that dogs usually need to relieve themselves at specific times, and that if dogs get used to going at certain times, that is when they will always want to go. We know enough about digestion to know that most puppies have to relieve themselves about 15 to 30 minutes after eating. Puppies also typically have to go right after they wake up, and following vigorous play sessions. Use this information to your advantage and set up a schedule.

Remember to go outside with your puppy, at least for the first few months, and praise to the skies when he does his business in the appropriate place. That message will come through loud and clear. When your puppy begins to ask to go outside by waiting

Don't scold your puppy if he makes a mistake inside the house.

Instructor vs. Trainer

Obedience instructors teach people and pets how to communicate through the language of training. In other words, an obedience instructor teaches you how to train your dog. Sometimes people say "trainer" when they really mean "obedience instructor," but technically, a trainer trains your dog for you, then gives him back to you. This isn't very common anymore. The best way to build your relationship is to train your pet yourself, so look for an obedience instructor that can guide you in how to do this.

or pawing at the door, you can feel proud to know that you have communicated the rules, and your Golden Retriever has chosen to follow them.

TYPES OF TRAINING

Essentially, training your Golden Retriever is really learning a mutual language. Training isn't just taking your Golden Retriever to a training class once each week, although this is one important component of training. Training a dog is a way to establish guidelines for living together. In its more advanced form, it can become a tool for teaching your Golden Retriever how to compete in canine sports, learn service work, or do other complex tasks.

No matter how far you want to take training, however, it starts with a few basic commands, consistent application, and the establishment of some ground rules. Training is something you can do with your dog every single day. The more you train, the more you and your Golden Retriever will grow to understand each other, and that is one of the most important ways to make your relationship with your pet a satisfying and happy one.

TRAINING GOALS

To help you get a clear picture of exactly what you want out of training your Golden Retriever, it helps to set some goals first. Do you want a dog who behaves in the house, or are you looking for more advanced training? Before you choose a training path—a method, a class, a trainer—answer these questions about what you expect from your Golden Retriever:

- What are the house rules for dogs in your home? Do you want to enforce a no-dogs-on-the-furniture rule, or is a Golden on the couch just fine with you? Is it important to you that your Golden stays away from the dinner table at mealtime, or do you prefer a dog who will "clean up" the occasional spilled crumbs? What about outside time? Do you want your dog to spend a lot of time in the fresh air in a fenced garden, or do you want a dog who will spend most of his time inside? Consider what your personal priorities are for dog behaviour, in the house and in the garden, and write these down. Knowing what you expect from your dog from the start will help you to target your training.
- What other kinds of activities will you do with your Golden Retriever? Consider whether you will travel frequently with

Look for a trainer who uses positive reinforcement in the form of treats, toys, and praise to reward dogs.

your Golden, hike, swim in lakes, or go for long runs or bike rides that require top condition. Would you like your Golden Retriever to compete in canine sports like agility, flyball or canine freestyle. Are you interested in the show scene, or competitive obedience?

- Maybe you would like to get into therapy work, taking your Golden Retriever to nursing homes or hospitals to visit patients and residents. This can impact the kind of training you do.
- Some Golden Retrievers have a special talent for assistance work working with the disabled. Others are aces at search and rescue, drug detection, bomb detection, or police work. These activities require highly specialised training from a young age, and it is generally a job for professional trainers. Could this kind of activity be for you?

Finding a Class and an Obedience Instructor

Once you have a clear idea of your expectations, you can start to build your Golden Retriever's training team. You are the coach, and you get to decide who will assist in helping your Golden Retriever to become his best self. The first person to "recruit" for your team is a professional obedience instructor who holds dog training classes.

Dog training classes aren't just for fun. They serve several critical functions. The first level, often called "puppy class" or "puppy socialisation," introduces your puppy to many other people and dogs in a friendly, controlled environment—a crucial part of socialisation. Basic obedience classes go on to teach the meaning of some basic cues: sit, down, stay, come, and heel, for example. These cues are the building blocks for more advanced obedience moves, as well as training for sports, therapy, tracking, and other doggy work and play activities.

Advanced obedience classes build on these basics, chaining cues one after the other to teach more complex manoeuvres, more patience, and more self-control. Specialised classes teach obedience activities such as formal obedience competition, how to run an agility course, how to run a flyball race, how to "dance" in a canine freestyle competition, or how to compete in a conformation dog show. Advanced training can also target specialised disciplines, such as field trials and working trials.

Most areas have at least one dog obedience instructor, and some have dog obedience clubs that offer training classes. You can ask your veterinary surgeon for recommendations, or look up "dog training" in the phone book to find what is available in your area. Make sure you always visit a class before signing up, and meet the instructor. It is best to go along without your dog. You want to be sure you like and agree with the training style.

Training Styles

Obedience instructors may prefer any number of training styles, but most fall into one of two categories: traditional and contemporary. Traditional trainers often use choke chains and punishment to teach a dog how to follow commands. Contemporary trainers emphasise positive reinforcement and rewards for following cues.

Most contemporary trainers feel that dogs learn faster and the dog-human relationship grows stronger with positive reinforcement training rather than with punitive training. They focus on rewarding the dogs when they do the right thing, in order to communicate what the owner wants or needs the dog to do. Dogs work hard to get rewards, so this method works very well for most pets. Contemporary training classes also often focus on socialising

To get the most out of training your Golden, it's important to set some goals.

puppies and on teaching pet owners how to teach good house manners and solve behavioural problems like barking and jumping up. A good trainer will be happy to answer any questions you have about dog-human relations, and give you strategies to make your relationship with your Golden Retriever work.

Because Golden Retrievers are a sensitive, agreeable, and tractable breed, contemporary training methods are the preferred training method for them. No need to yank them around. Just praise them when they get it right, and you'll have a happy Golden Retriever, eager to please you.

Talk to your instructor about his or her methods, and also, see for yourself. Some things to consider when talking to an obedience instructor and observing a class:

- Obedience instructors should be good with dogs and humans. Remember, the instructor is teaching you how to train your dog. Do you feel free to ask questions, and do you get clear answers that make sense? Look for someone with good communication skills.
- Is the class well organised? Do people seem to understand what they are supposed to do?
- Is the class in a large, well-ventilated space, with room for everyone? Are people required to pick up after their dogs?
- Do you learn something just by watching the class? Do you like the teacher when you talk to her, and feel like she really knows what she is doing?
- Are all the dogs friendly, or at least, under control? Or do you feel that any of the dogs seem to be dangerous, or putting other dogs at risk? Just because that 150-pound Rottweiler looks scary doesn't mean he is. He might become your Golden's new best buddy! But any dog of any size that growls, lunges, and bites, should not be allowed in a class with other dogs.
- Does the teacher use positive reinforcement in the form of treats, toys, and praise to reward dogs? Or, does the teacher use punishment, like jerking a chain collar or swatting the dog? For Golden Retrievers, avoid trainers that use the latter approach.

Clicker Training

Clicker training is a popular training method that uses a small plastic device with a button that makes a loud clicking sound. Clicker training precisely marks a behaviour, so your dog knows exactly what you are rewarding. It works well for training very specific behaviours, like touching a target or teaching the steps in a complicated trick.

Clicker training works so well because the click is a short, sharp sound that marks a behaviour much more precisely than a treat or saying "good dog." The click almost exactly coincides with the desired behaviour, so there is no doubt what you want. Try it and you might just be astounded at how quickly dogs pick up the concept. Eventually, you won't always offer a treat because just knowing they have done what you wanted is, in itself, a reward for Goldens. Golden Retrievers typically respond very well to clicker training, and many obedience instructors offer clicker training classes.

Here is how clicker training works:

- First, you "load" the clicker. Show your Golden Retriever the clicker. Click it, and immediately give your Golden Retriever a small treat. Do this several times, during several different sessions, every day for three days to a week. You are teaching your Golden Retriever that the sound of a click equals a treat.
- Next, use the clicker to mark a behaviour your Golden Retriever already knows, such as sit. Deliver the verbal cue. The instant your Golden Retriever sits, click the clicker, then offer a treat. Repeat often.
- Now, you can use the clicker to mark behaviours your Golden Retriever doesn't yet know. For example, maybe you want to train your Golden Retriever to jump up for a treat. Hold up a treat. Try to lure your Golden Retriever to jump. Goldens will typically start offering different behaviours, to see what will score the treat. The instant he does the behaviour you want, click, then give him the treat.

Once your Golden Retriever understands that a click marks exactly what you want, he will start offering behaviours to try to get the click (which to him then means he will get a reward). Use it to train advanced behaviours, including competitive obedience moves, navigating agility equipment, or doing complicated tricks like turning on the light switch or ringing a bell to go outside.

Pocket Full 'O Treats

Especially in the initial training stages, every family member should always carry a pocket full of treats. Then you are always ready to reward your Golden Retriever when he does something good, like sit or lie down on cue, or when he brings you something. Remember, always reward the retrieve!

"DIY" Training

Sometimes, people can't or don't want to take their dogs to obedience classes. Classes are a lot of fun, a great way to socialise a puppy, and a fun way to meet other dog owners. They are also incredibly valuable because they give you access to a professional obedience instructor who can help you to manage your Golden Retriever in person, with a hands-on approach. You can ask questions in person and when you aren't sure how to train something, the teacher can help you. But you can also train and socialise your Golden Retriever yourself. It just takes a little know-how.

The first step is to learn as much about dog training as you can. Read books about dog training, read magazine articles that tackle

The entire family should be involved in your Golden Retriever's training.

training issues, and talk to other people who train their dogs. Then, start training your Golden Retriever from the very beginning, making training practice a fun and enjoyable part of your daily routine. A few things to keep in mind if you choose to train your Golden Retriever on your own:

- Training should always be fun. If you or your dog isn't having a good time, training won't be nearly as effective. Goldens are highly motivated to spend time with you, to play, and to work for treats, toys, and praise. If you or your dog is getting frustrated, take a break and pick it up again later.
- Train every day, once or twice, for short periods, rather than one long training session every week. You'll both have more fun and your Golden Retriever will learn much faster.
- Puppies can easily learn to sit, lie down, stay, come, and walk on a lead. Older dogs can learn more advanced commands, but teach them one step at a time, solidifying each step before moving on. Don't be in a rush to accomplish too much, too soon. Better to let your Golden Retriever be successful than to set him up for failure.
- Use the Golden Retriever's natural instincts for easier training.

Anything that requires retrieving and carrying something by mouth will feel very natural to your Golden. Anything that has anything to do with a ball will probably be a lot of fun for everyone.

- Always, always, always praise your Golden when he brings you anything at all, even things he isn't supposed to have. If you scold the retrieve, he will learn to take things and hide with them rather than fessing up. If you praise the retrieve, you can teach your Golden Retriever to bring you almost anything at all. Goldens have learned to fetch the remote control, find the car keys, even sort the laundry. Always, always, always praise the retrieve!
- Set training goals. One great goal is to train your Golden Retriever to earn his Canine Good Citizen certification (see Chapter 7).

Training With the Whole Family

One of the reasons you might want to train your Golden Retriever yourself, rather than sending him off to a professional trainer, is because you are the one who will be living with your Golden Retriever every day. Training is how you and your Golden Retriever communicate, and you both need to practice this "language" every day. If you aren't the only person living in your home, other family members should train your Golden Retriever, too. Even small children can train Golden Retrievers, with supervision.

Dogs are smart, and they quickly learn who they have to listen to, and who they can get away with ignoring completely. If your Golden Retriever thinks that when you say, "Sit," it means "sit," but when your child says, "Sit," it means "jump up and knock down the short little human," you have a problem. Get the whole family involved in training from the start, and your Golden Retriever will love that everyone is involved in the fun "game" you call "training."

If every family member spends a little time each day training your Golden Retriever, you are also getting the benefit of multiple training sessions for faster learning. Here are some fun family games to get everyone involved, and to quickly teach your Golden Retriever some basics.

Training Tip

Train for short periods every day instead of one long training session once a week.

There are lots of fun retrieving games you can play with your Golden.

Golden Circle

This exercise works best for young puppies, and it teaches the cue "come," a very important cue for your Golden Retriever to master. While teaching come, this exercise also teaches your Golden that this cue can come from anyone in the family.

To prepare, first give everybody a few treats. Hide the treats in your hand or in a pocket. Next, have everyone in the family sit in a circle, knees or feet touching, with your Golden Retriever in the middle. This works best for young puppies because a larger dog could easily just choose to leave the circle, and depending on how many people you have, a larger dog could be too big to fit easily in the circle.

Now, choose a word that you want to signify "come." This might be "come," "here," or anything else everyone will remember and use. Family members should take turns calling your Golden Retriever, randomly. When your Golden comes to the person who is calling him, that person should immediately give him a little treat, praise him, and pet him.

Here's the tricky part. Everybody else in the circle who is not calling the dog must remain stone-faced and should display no indication of having any treats. If the Golden goes to anyone

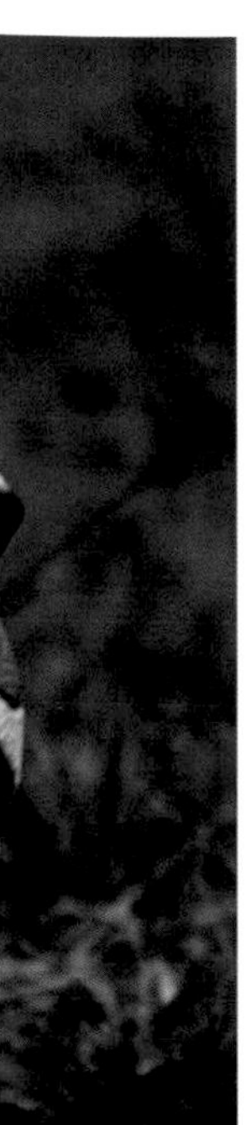

who is not calling him, ignore him completely. Don't even make eye contact. Don't worry, this isn't mean. You are teaching your Golden to focus on the person who is saying that all-important cue word. Your turn will come. Keep randomly calling the dog. Your Golden loves attention and treats, so he will quickly learn to dash to the person dispensing both those great rewards.

Do this exercise once or twice a day for at least a week. Then you can continue to reinforce the come command in other ways, too, such as using the method described later in this chapter in the section on basic obedience.

Happy Retriever

Always praise the retrieve. This is a key concept for every single family member to understand. If your Golden Retriever brings your daughter her slightly chewed favourite toy, shrieks of horror are not the proper response, even if that is how your daughter feels. The same goes for a chewed favourite shoe, glove, or unfortunate rodent from the garden. But Golden Retrievers can quickly learn which items you prefer them to retrieve. Here is a game that will help to reinforce this. This game also helps to teach your Golden Retriever the exact names of acceptable chew items. Anybody in the family can play this game with your Golden Retriever, and you can all play it at once, taking turns asking for particular items. Here is how it works:

Phase One:

- First, select three different items your Golden Retriever is allowed to chew. Don't use old shoes or old toys that resemble new shoes and new toys you don't want your Golden to chew. Instead, use a selection of your Golden's toys, but all three should look different (for example, a Nylabone, a stuffable toy, and a tennis ball). Put these in the centre of the room.
- Chances are, the mere presence of the toys will get your Golden Retriever interested, and he might grab one and bring it to you right away. If so, praise him and say the name of the toy. If he doesn't, give your Golden Retriever a specific command: "Get the ball." No matter what your Golden Retriever brings you, praise him, but say the name of the toy. If he brings you the toy you ask for, really lay on that praise!

Games involving sit are fun and easy for your puppy.

- Repeat this until your Golden Retriever understands that you want him to bring you something.

  Phase Two:
- Now the game gets harder. Ask for a particular toy, and if your Golden Retriever brings you the wrong one, ignore him. Don't scold, just look away, but repeat the cue: "Get the ball." Note: *This is the only time when you can get away with not praising the retrieve!* But you aren't scolding the retrieve, either. You are just ignoring it.
- Goldens like to try different behaviours until they get the right

one. Wait until he brings you the right toy. Then praise like crazy! It won't take your Golden long to learn the names of those three toys.

- Repeat often. Golden Retrievers think this is great fun, and kids will enjoy it, too.

Phase Three:

- By this phase, your Golden Retriever should understand this game well enough to separate retrieving from chewing, so you can add other toys and items to the mix. This time, put three different things in the middle of the room.
- Golden Retrievers love to try to work out which thing you want and what will elicit the praise. As before, ignore your Golden until he brings you the right thing, then really lay it on thick.
- Repeat often. Everyone in the family should do this frequently. Pretty soon, your Golden Retriever will have a big vocabulary, and you'll be laying the groundwork for a host of clever retrieving tricks.

The Sit Game

Golden Retrievers love kids, but in their exuberance, they can get a little too rough. Puppies like to try to gnaw flailing little fingers, and that big tail can knock over a toddler with one enthusiastic wag. But kids can quickly train Golden Retrievers with the Sit Game.

This game is easy, and quickly teaches your Golden Retriever that it is more rewarding to sit nicely for a small child than to jump on a small child. This requires some training of both Golden Retriever and child, however. Here's what to do:

- First, as you are training your Golden Retriever, help your kids remember that they should always carry treats with them, in a handy pocket or waist pack. Remind kids that they should never, ever give the dog a treat without asking him to do something first, and the dog should not be able to get at the treats himself.
- Now, at every possible opportunity, kids should ask the dog to sit. Getting up in the morning, before breakfast, before leaving for school, when coming home from school, after dinner, before bed—whenever your child comes into contact with your Golden Retriever, have him first deliver the cue: "sit." As soon as the Golden Retriever sits, the child gives him a treat.

Games for Kids

Use the Sit Game to get your children involved in training.

Teaching your Golden the down command is useful in competitive obedience.

- It may take a few tries and some intervention from you at the beginning for your Golden Retriever to figure out that when your child says, "Sit," he means it, and that he will not be handing out any goodies until the dog sits nicely. Kids may be tempted to give treats for half a sit, or a brief sit and then a jumping up to get the treat, but supervise initially until both child and dog understand that the dog doesn't get a treat until he sits, and that he will have to stay sitting to actually get the treat.
- Once your child has this down, give your child a treat! (But not a dog biscuit.)

Statue

This final tip isn't really a game, but more of a strategy. When faced with a jumping dog, kids tend to get very excited—either happily or in fear—and jump around, waving their arms. This just gets dogs even more excited, so much so that they may not even notice that the child is telling them to sit, or is not happy with the jumping.

Instead, teach your children to be a statue when faced with an exuberant dog. The child should stand completely still, arms folded, fingers tucked in. Do not make eye contact with the dog. Do not move. When the child ceases to be exciting and interesting, the dog will usually calm down, at least until an adult can intervene. When the dog is calm, the child can then say, "Sit," and offer a treat when the dog is able to listen.

BASIC OBEDIENCE

Basic obedience is the term trainers and instructors use to refer to a few basic cues dogs can learn, which you can then build upon in many ways. Basic obedience cues set the stage for good manners, for an agreeable companion, and for learning more advanced behaviours, from cute tricks to important jobs. A dog with this basic repertoire is akin to a piano player who has mastered his scales, or a person learning the basic grammar of a new language.

In competitive obedience, these cues form the basis for what dogs must do to compete in the first levels of obedience competition. The point behind competitive obedience was, originally, the same as the point behind dog training in general: to help dogs become ideal human companions. Whether you choose to compete in obedience competition or not, teach your dog these basics and you'll be ready for anything.

Sit

Sit is one of the easiest cues to teach, and one of the most useful. A dog who is sitting cannot be jumping up on you, running out the front door, or pulling on a lead. Most people would rather encounter a dog who is sitting, friendly tail wagging, than a dog who wants to jump on them, so the sit command can make a big difference in how well your dog gets along with others. Sitting is also the basis for teaching the stay command. Once your dog knows the sit command, use it often. Dogs who sit before getting a treat, sit before you put the food bowl down, sit when someone comes in the front door, and sit as the first and last exercise in a training session will tend to offer this behaviour frequently, in the hopes that it will result in a reward.

Even very young puppies can learn to sit. You can probably successfully teach this to your Golden Retriever the very first day he comes home to live with you. Your breeder might already have taught this to the puppies! The easiest way to teach "sit" is to lure your dog into position with a treat, then reward the behaviour, immediately linking it with the verbal cue. Here's how:

- Sit next to your puppy with a small treat in your hand.

Sit Troubleshooting Tip

If your puppy just doesn't want to sit down, you can gently fold his back legs down and guide him physically into a sit, to help him. As you do this, say, "Sit."

- Hold the treat directly in front of the puppy's nose, so he can see and smell it, but don't let him have it yet.
- Slowly raise the treat in an arc, over the nose and eyes, so your puppy follows the treat by looking up.
- When puppies look up, they naturally sit down. If he sits, say, "Sit" as he is sitting, then immediately give him the treat.
- If he tries to turn around, put the treat back in front of his nose. Keep luring his head up until he sits. As soon as he sits, give him the treat and praise him!
- Repeat often. Golden Retrievers understand this cue quickly.

Down

Down is another useful command. A dog lying down can learn to stay in this position for a long time, called the "long down." This can be helpful if you don't want your Golden Retriever nosing around in people's laps during dinner looking for scraps, or if you want him to lie down and relax while you are working at your computer or watching television. The down and long down are also useful exercises in competitive obedience, and a dog who can do this easily should have no problem when attempting to earn his Good Citizen award. Teach "down" after you have mastered "sit." Here's how to teach down:

- Give your puppy the cue to sit.
- Put a treat in front of his nose, then draw it forward and down, in a diagonal line away from the puppy and towards the ground. Move the treat slowly.
- Most puppies will move forward and down towards the treat, into a down. As he is lying down, say, "Down."
- If your puppy tries to stand up and walk forward to the treat, keep a hand on his backside to keep it in a sitting position. Don't move the treat so far forward that he can't reach it just by lying down.
- As soon as he is down, give him the treat and praise and pet him.

Down Troubleshooting Tip

Some dogs resist lying all the way down. They like to try to hover just above the ground without actually relaxing into a full down, just in case they need to spring back up again quickly. This is especially common in active puppies. Don't give the treat for the partial down. Keep luring and physically guiding your dog all the way down as you say, "Down." It can help to move his front paws into a down position. When he is fully on the floor, reward him.

Stay

Stay is one of the most important cues your Golden can learn. It can keep him safe and under control near traffic and other hazardous situations. It can also help to keep him under control in the home, a crucial part of living with humans. Make sure your Golden knows "sit" first. Teaching "stay" is easiest with two people, but you can do it by yourself, too. Here is how to teach "stay":

- Clip a lead on your puppy and give your puppy the sit cue. Praise him for sitting. Have a family member or friend sit with him, lightly holding his lead.
- Sit or stand in front of your puppy, about 3 feet away. Hold up your hand, palm facing the puppy, and say, "Stay." Wait. If your puppy stays for three seconds, have the person holding the puppy praise him and give him a treat. Also, come back to the puppy when he stays to praise him yourself, too. You want to reinforce to the puppy that he should stay, not that he should stay and then come to get the treat. This is too confusing at first. If you are teaching this alone, then give the treat yourself, but do it by coming to the puppy, not by letting him come to you to get the treat. Again, coming to you breaks the stay. (You aren't teaching the come command right now.)
- Repeat this several times.
- If the puppy tries to come to you, the person holding him should not restrain him with the lead. Let him try to come to you, but turn away from him and ignore him. Don't even look at him. Have the other person call the puppy back or guide him back with the lead and sit again. (Always praise a good sit.)
- Repeat step #2. Keep doing this until your puppy understands that coming to you gets nothing, but staying gets rewarded.
- Repeat many times until the puppy reliably stays every time.
- Now, move back about 6 feet and do this again, in exactly the same way. Repeat often until the puppy reliably stays every time.
- Now, hold the stay longer, up to one minute. Repeat often.
- Gradually increase the distance and the time of the stay. Eventually, move out of sight for the stay.
- Finally, practice the stay in many different ways, a few times every day. Sometimes, have your puppy sit and stay, sometimes have him lie down and stay. Have him stay for short periods and long periods, while you are close or while you are far away. Keep him guessing about how long the stay will be. Golden Retrievers think this is fun!

Stay Troubleshooting Tip

Always come to your Golden Retriever after the stay, rather than calling him to you, until he fully understands the stay cue. Always ignore your Golden Retriever completely if he breaks the stay. Even saying "No!" is attention, and more rewarding than being ignored. Golden Retrievers hate to be ignored and will do just about anything to get your attention, so make sure you give your attention for the behaviours you want.

Come

Come is a similarly important safety exercise as well as a convenient way to collect your Golden Retriever when you need him. Because Goldens are retrievers and instinctually bring things to you, this cue is

For the stay command, hold up your hand, palm facing your Golden, and say, "Stay."

easier for them than for some other breeds that tend to go off on their own. A Golden Retriever who always comes when called can be trusted off-lead during dog activities like agility competitions, or on hikes and walks away from traffic areas. Goldens who come when called are also safer, because you can stop them from getting into trouble if they are headed towards traffic or some other danger. You can also put others at ease who might be afraid of dogs in general if they see that you can always call your Golden Retriever and he will come to you and not towards them. (Yes, some people are even nervous about Golden Retrievers!) A dog that comes when called is definitely a good citizen and makes a good impression on the public. Practice this command every single day, as often as you can, no matter how much you think your Golden Retriever gets it. Again, this is easier to teach with another person, but you can do it alone, too. Before teaching the come command, your puppy should know how to sit. Here's how to teach it:

- Clip a lead on your puppy and give him the cue to sit.
- Have a friend or family member sit with the puppy, but you take the lead.
- Either give your puppy the cue to stay, or just have the person with the puppy gently hook a finger in his collar to keep him in place.
- Holding the lead, walk away from your puppy, the length of the lead. Turn to face the puppy.

- Call the puppy to you, using your chosen cue word, such as "come" or "here."
- Most puppies will come. If yours does, immediately give him a treat and praise him. If he doesn't, gently guide him towards you with the lead (don't yank him, though), then reward him when he comes.
- If he won't come to you, or is distracted by something else, try again later. Don't force your puppy to come. That's no fun and can have the wrong effect.
- Repeat often, calling your puppy to you at random times during the day and rewarding him enthusiastically whenever he comes.
- Also, remember the exercise using the whole family, earlier in this chapter, called "Golden Circle"? This is another great way to reinforce the come cue.

LEAD TRAINING

The world is big and exciting, so what eager Golden Retriever wouldn't want to barrel down the street in search of adventure, especially when he has a handy lead by which to drag you along behind him? Some Golden Retrievers walk nicely on a lead without pulling, but most of those had to learn how. Walking on a lead isn't natural behaviour for dogs, but because we need to keep them safe from cars and other hazards, it is a necessity of modern life. So, how do you teach your Golden Retriever to stop pulling and walk next to you?

At first, a new puppy who has never walked on a lead may not understand what you want him to do. Begin with very short sessions, clipping a light nylon lead onto your puppy's buckle collar. Hold the lead and let the puppy walk around the house or garden at the end of the lead. You can try some verbal cues at this time, too. Have your puppy sit, walk away the length of the lead, then call your puppy to you. Reward him with a treat. As often as you can in these early weeks, make it rewarding for a puppy on a lead to pay attention to you and what you are doing.

The first trick to getting your Golden Retriever to walk nicely on a lead is to keep his attention on you, as opposed to pigeons waddling beside the pond in the park or the Fox Terrier in the neighbour's garden. Easier said than done! Golden Retrievers, especially puppies, are fascinated by all the things to see, hear, smell, and roll in that they could encounter on a walk. That's why

Come Troubleshooting Tip

It's easy to confuse this training cue with the stay cue. If the puppy has to stay to wait for you to move away and say, "Come," everyone can get a little mixed up about just what is being rewarded. Practice the come command throughout the day, when your puppy isn't paying attention to you. Say, "Come," randomly, and whenever your puppy comes to you, give him a treat (you have that pocketful of treats, right?).

they like walks so much. You and your pocket of treats might interest them when nothing else is going on, but how can you compete with those giggling children down the road or that bird chirping and teasing from the tree branch above?

You can, but it helps to start early. Even before you venture around the block, you can begin to reinforce how to walk nicely on the lead. In the garden or in the house, hold a handful of small treats. Hold the lead, with the puppy standing on one side of you (it doesn't really matter which side). Step forward and say some verbal cue (always use the same word), such as "walk," "come on," or "let's go." Keep the treat visible so your puppy sees it and wants to follow it. If he walks with you, even for just a few feet, praise him and give him the treat. These mini walks, of 5 or 6 feet, are laying the groundwork for longer walks. Increase the distance in very small bits, so your Golden Retriever has lots of chances to succeed at, and be rewarded for, walking next to you while paying attention to you.

It all comes down to one basic concept: You have to make walking on a lead without pulling more rewarding than walking on a lead with pulling. This will take some patience on your part, but it can be done. Remember, start small. Practise a lot. And don't give your Golden Retriever any rewards at all for pulling on the lead. Here is a lead-walking game to practice this. You can do this in the house, in the garden, or while walking down the street. Practice it often!

- Begin with your Golden Retriever on a lead, standing beside you. Have treats.
- Say the verbal cue, "walk" (or whatever), then begin walking, with treats in view.
- If your Golden Retriever walks with you, occasionally give him a small treat as you go, praising him as he is walking next to you without pulling.
- If your Golden Retriever begins to pull, stop walking. Stand perfectly still and look away. This is, obviously, not what your Golden Retriever had in mind when he was trying to pull. He wanted to go faster, not stop. Ignore him completely until he stops pulling, which he will eventually do as he tries to work out what you want from him.
- As soon as he stops pulling, get his attention again. Praise him. Say the cue for walk, and begin walking.

- The second he starts pulling again, stop walking. Yes, continue this routine for the entire duration of the walk. You might not get very far. The first time, you might not even get down the driveway! That's just fine. The point of this exercise is not to cover vast mileage, but to train your Golden Retriever that if he is going to pull on the lead, he is not going to get very far. If he walks nicely beside you, on the other hand, he will not only get praise and an occasional treat, but he will also get to keep walking!

This exercise takes a lot of patience, and many people get frustrated and stop doing it too soon. It may take days, even weeks of patient refusal to move when your dog pulls, but it really does work. Golden Retrievers work very hard to get rewards. The dog pulling his owner down the street is getting rewarded for pulling. He's getting to forge ahead! As soon as your dog understands that pulling is not rewarding, but walking nicely is very rewarding, he'll get it.

UNDESIRABLE DOG BEHAVIOURS AND PROBLEM BEHAVIOURS

A well-trained and well-socialised dog is much less likely to exhibit problem behaviours, but most pet owners have to deal

The first trick to getting your Golden Retriever to walk nicely on a lead is to keep his attention on you.

Goldens need both physical and mental activity to be healthy.

with a few behaviours they don't care for and want to redirect. Problem behaviours and typical dog behaviours aren't exactly the same thing. Undesirable dog behaviours are those behaviours that are perfectly normal and natural for dogs, but that are not pleasing to humans and don't work well in human society. Problem behaviours, on the other hand, are behaviours that result when your dog has a problem, such as fear, anxiety, or aggression.

But almost any behaviour humans don't like, whether digging and chewing or barking and growling, can be largely resolved by doing just three simple things. These are things all pet owners probably know they should do anyway, but unfortunately, many people neglect them. They are:

- Giving your dog enough attention
- Giving your dog enough exercise
- Giving your dog a job to do

Golden Retrievers are smart, active, curious, friendly, sociable creatures. They need lots of activity, both mental and physical. They need to have a "pack" to hang out with. And this natural-born working breed needs a job to do. If you don't provide your dog with these three essentials, you will have problems. That goes for

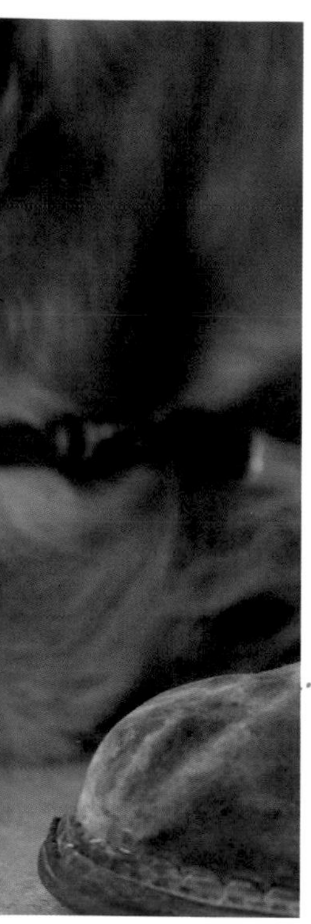

any breed, but particularly for the super-social and super-active Golden Retriever.

If you are having a behaviour problem you might be able to solve it by increasing your dog's exercise regime and by increasing the time you spend with your dog. That includes time training, grooming, playing, walking, driving in the car together, or just hanging out, watching television. That's why you have a dog, isn't it? Exercise your Golden, and do it together. You'll both be healthier, and behaviour problems might just disappear.

However, exercise and attention don't solve every problem or inconvenient canine behaviour, so here are some additional targeted tips for tackling behaviours that don't mesh with life in the human world.

Chewing

Retrievers are mouthy. They like to chew, they like to carry things in their mouths, and they like to use their mouths as a way to explore and manipulate the world. Some Golden Retrievers will even take their humans, hand in mouth, to lead them where they want to go. That means the chewing is a perfectly natural and normal dog behaviour, and a very common and necessary retriever behaviour. Chewing cannot and should not be stopped, but it can be managed. The trick is to give your Golden Retriever things that are just fine to chew, while teaching him that other things are off limits.

All puppies need to chew, and many adult Golden Retrievers continue to chew, while others prefer to have things to carry around in their mouths, but rarely destroy their toys. Provide your Golden Retriever with many toys, but don't put them out all at once. Rotate them every week or so, to keep things interesting.

If your Golden Retriever is chewing destructively, he either doesn't have appropriate things to chew, doesn't know what is appropriate to chew, or isn't getting enough exercise and attention. All these problems are up to you to solve. Increase your dog's exercise, spend more time with him, and give him more things to chew. Keep things you don't want your Golden Retriever to chew out of reach. (This is one good way to get your kids to keep their toys and clothes off the floor—clean it up or risk losing it!) Keep your shoes and clothes put

Chewing Troubleshooting Tip

If your Golden Retriever is chewing obsessively, he could be suffering from a medical problem. Some dogs chew excessively to relieve the stress of pain, discomfort, or anxiety. Check with your vet to be sure your Golden Retriever is in good health.

away, and if your Golden gets something you left out and chews it up, well…whose fault is that? Puppies are still learning.

Finally, as you are training your puppy about what to chew, always direct him to his tennis ball, Nylabone, or whatever is acceptable. If you catch him with something he isn't supposed to chew, firmly say "No," take it away, immediately replace it with an acceptable substitute, then praise your Golden when he chews the right thing. Some people like to keep a box, basket, or plastic tub of dog toys in easy reach, so your Golden can select something to chew whenever he feels the need.

Digging

Digging is just plain fun for dogs. It is good exercise, it is satisfying, and on a hot day, a nice dirt hole feels cool and refreshing. Some Goldens aren't diggers, but others really enjoy it. If this sounds like your dog, and you would prefer to keep your lawn, flowerbeds, and vegetable garden intact, consider these strategies:

All puppies need to chew, and many adult Golden Retrievers continue to chew throughout their lives.

- Increase your Golden's exercise. Many Goldens dig to burn off steam. Increase the time, length, and/or speed of daily walks and play sessions. A worn-out, properly stimulated Golden Retriever will be much less likely to dig trenches in the garden.
- Give your Golden a place to dig. A nice sandbox or plot of dirt just for your Golden can keep him out of your landscaping. When he starts to dig somewhere else, lead him over to his own digging spot and praise him when he digs there.
- Supervise! If you want to know what your dog is doing in the garden, go out there with him. Goldens often dig just because

To help ward off certain problem behaviours, make sure your dog gets a significant amount of exercise every single day.

they are bored. If you are out in the yard too, they won't be bored. If you go inside, your dog would probably rather be where you are, anyway.

- Plant your gardens and flowers outside the fenced garden. Keep your Golden Retriever inside the fenced garden.
- If your Golden Retriever is digging out and escaping, secure that fence. Line the base of the fence with bricks or pour cement.

Barking

Golden Retrievers aren't normally yappers, but Golden Retrievers left in the garden with nothing to do are likely to take up barking as a hobby. Insecure Goldens who aren't properly socialised may also tend to bark a lot more than they should, because they haven't learned that someone else will take care of things, and they don't have to worry so much about every person, animal, and blowing leaf that passes by. Anxiety, fear, stress, and a lack of exercise all can potentially contribute to excessive barking, and this bad habit is more than an annoyance to you. It could get you in serious trouble with your neighbours. Here are some strategies for handling an excessive barker:

- Don't leave your Golden Retriever alone in the garden if he is an excessive barker. Stay out there with him, or bring him inside.
- Don't reward barking! If you yell, "No, no, no!" at your Golden Retriever when he is barking, he might think you are barking with him, and see this as reinforcement, or at least justification.

If your Golden is an excessive barker, try teaching him to speak. If you give a cue "Speak" and then reward him, you are controlling his behaviour, and he will learn to bark on command rather than giving free reign to his feelings.

- Practise together. Sit with your Golden Retriever in the house or garden, and set up a situation where he will bark. Tell him, "Shhh," and when he doesn't bark, reward him. Dogs quickly pick up on what you mean. If the object of his barking is too exciting, however, he can forget you are even there. In this case, remove the dog from the situation until he calms down, then try again. Practice, practice, practice, and don't forget to reward the quiet behaviour.
- Close the curtains or put him in a room where he can't see people walking by.
- Work on socialising your Golden Retriever more vigorously. Take him to more places, expose him to more people, and be sure these experiences are safe and positive.
- Give your Golden Retriever more exercise! (Oh, did I already mention that?)
- Use a bark collar that sprays a fine mist of citronella whenever your dog barks. This redirects your dog's attention so he can recognise that you are telling him to stop barking. This is not a punishment but a distraction. Reward when he stops barking. Mentioned in past books as negative.

Jumping Up

The key to curing Golden Retrievers who are always jumping on people is to teach them to sit. Isolate the events that trigger your Golden Retriever to jump up, and specifically work on setting up an automatic sit in those situations. For example, if your Golden Retriever always jumps on people when they come to the door, teach your Golden to come with you to the door (he wants to be involved!), then sit before you open it. If he jumps up, he gets no attention. If he sits, he gets a treat.

You can set this up by giving a friend some treats, then having them come to the door and ring the doorbell. Have your Golden sit. If he sits, and stays sitting, when the visitor comes in, have the visitor give him treats. If he jumps up, barks, and otherwise acts up, instruct your visitor to turn his or her back and completely ignore the dog. Have the visitor go outside and do it again. Do this often with different people. You are teaching your Golden that if he sits when someone rings the doorbell, he might get a treat. If he jumps on them, he gets ignored.

If your Golden Retriever jumps up on people while playing—common with children, who tend to get dogs very excited—you can train your Golden (and the children) by again setting up the situation for practice. Have kids constantly deliver the verbal cue, "Sit," and reward the dog when he sits. Encourage children not to reward jumping up by standing completely still and ignoring the dog when he jumps. Goldens are smart. They will get it if you are consistent and practice this often.

Escapee

Most Golden Retrievers won't try to run away unless they are scared, really bored, or enticed out by someone. Goldens want to be with you, but they also need stimulation, exercise, and company. No dog is happy left alone in the garden all day, and no dog should be left alone in the garden when you are gone. Keep your dog with you and keep him well exercised, and he should be more than happy to stay close to home. If you have to leave your Golden Retriever at home, leave him inside where he is safe.

Anxiety

Most Golden Retrievers who are well socialised and well trained won't suffer from anxiety, but anxiety is a more common problem with rescued Golden Retrievers, or those dogs who have suffered some kind of trauma, abandonment, or abuse. In some cases, a medical problem or injury can result in anxiety. In other cases, anxiety is more a dramatic reaction to you going away (often called "separation anxiety").

Signs of anxiety include excessive barking, destruction, panic, extreme fear, and fear biting. Some dogs may suffer anxiety during certain events, like a thunderstorm, during which they may pace, pant, shake, or hide. You might not be able to find any reason why your dog is afraid of something, but the signs of fear and anxiety

The key to curing Golden Retrievers who are always jumping on people is to teach them to sit.

are obvious. Some dogs suffer anxiety whenever left alone, or when the regular routine changes. These are often signs of a dog who has been abandoned or abused in the past, or simply of a dog that isn't very well socialised and doesn't adjust well to change.

Anxiety is a slippery problem, and not everybody agrees about how to address it. Because the problem could be medical, the first step is to see your veterinary surgeon and describe the symptoms in detail. In severe cases, vets may prescribe medicine to help calm the dog, in order to then treat the anxiety. If the dog checks out as healthy, consider consulting an animal behaviour specialist who can give you very specific strategies for dealing with this problem.

Anxiety is not something to be taken lightly. Not only is it extremely stressful for your dog, but it could result in aggressive behaviour, possibly putting other people, as well as your dog, at risk. This is why anxiety is best managed by professionals specifically trained in anxiety cases. But you can do some additional things to alleviate anxiety in your dog, too.

- Anxious dogs often have anxious owners. Try to be calm, relaxed, and casual around your dog, especially during events that are likely to trigger anxiety. Many dogs get very anxious and upset when their humans leave, but we don't make it any easier when we make a big deal about leaving, getting emotional and pouring attention on our dogs. This is actually very stressful for dogs. If your dog gets anxious when you leave, put him in his crate or area where he stays when you are gone about 15 minutes before you leave. Casually say good-bye if you must, then go about your business getting ready. Walk out without incident. Don't say anything! You will be telling your dog that when you leave, it is no big deal.
- When you come back home, also act casually. Come in, put down your things, check your messages, open the door of the crate, then address your dog casually. "Oh, hello there!" The less emotional you get about transitions, the more your dog will feel they aren't such a big deal, and he might begin to relax.
- Also, you can practice leaving. Without making a big deal about it, leave the house, then come back in just a few minutes. Do this often, to get him used to the fact that you leave, but always come back soon. This will also build his confidence.
- For anxiety during other events, again, try not to get all emotional. Dogs pick up on our emotions and you can promote a calm, relaxed, nonanxious environment by your behaviour. Or,

Jumping Up Troubleshooting Tip

While you are working on teaching your Golden not to jump on people, keep his lead on inside the house (when he is supervised), so that whenever a jumping trigger occurs, you can get immediate control over the dog and help him to succeed in controlling himself. Self-discipline often grows out of externally assisted discipline (just as true for kids as it is for dogs!). Also, if you have company over and you don't have the time or ability at the moment to use the situation as a training opportunity, put your Golden Retriever in his crate for some downtime. Better to remove the opportunity to jump up than to allow your Golden Retriever to make a mistake when you aren't able to do much about it.

Don't hesitate to consult a professional if your dog is showing signs of anxiety.

you can encourage such an environment.

- Finally, in the case of severe anxiety, please don't hesitate to consult a professional animal behaviour specialist, who can help and advise you. This is particularly important if your dog is injuring himself, destroying your property, or being aggressive in any way.

How to Find an Animal Behaviour Specialist

People don't often think about calling an animal behaviour specialist until a problem is very advanced. They see a vet, an obedience instructor, and they may ask questions of the local pet store employee, but what about a behaviour specialist? What are they, and where do you find a good one?

There are several types of animal behaviour specialists:

- Any trainer can call him or herself an "animal behaviour consultant," which doesn't require any kind of degree or certification. Some of these trainers specialise in problem behaviours, primarily because they have a lot of experience with them. But because they don't have to have any particular credentials, consult with these animal behaviour specialists with care, and be sure to get recommendations.
- The Association of Pet Behaviour Counsellors (APBC) is a UK-based organisation that holds details of APBC counsellors. Check out their website at www.apbc.org.uk. In most cases, you will need a referral from your vet and then you can make an appointment with a counsellor.

If your Golden Retriever is having a behaviour problem, such as severe anxiety or aggression, that requires professional help, talk to your vet about referring you to a good animal behaviour specialist.

Chapter 7

ADVANCED TRAINING AND ACTIVITIES

With Your Golden Retriever

If you want to get serious about competitive sports, dog shows, or other advanced training, you picked the right breed. Golden Retrievers are easy to train, and a well-trained Golden Retriever versed in the basics of obedience are just as pleasurable to train for performance activities.

Advanced training is a Golden Retriever's dream job. Driven to work, pining to spend time with you, and naturally energetic, Golden Retrievers seem almost custom made for dog sports and competition. Always gorgeous in the show ring, playfully precise in the obedience ring, enthusiastic and nimble on the agility course, speedy and coordinated in a flyball race, joyfully driven in field work, and almost psychic when it comes to therapy and service work, Golden Retrievers show their true colours when you make the most of their natural abilities.

CANINE GOOD CITIZEN

This is a scheme run by the Kennel Club that is designed to reward dogs who have good manners at home and in the community. The programme stresses responsible pet ownership for owners and basic good manners for dogs.

The scheme was lauched in 1992. Since then, over 52,000 dogs have passed the test, which is administered through more than 1,000 training organisations.

Any dog is eligible to take part in the Good Citizen Dog Scheme, which is a noncompetitive plan that trains owners and dogs for everyday situations. There are four awards—bronze, silver, gold, and puppy foundation assessment—which are based on the level of training that both dog and owner have reached together.

For more information, contact the Kennel Club at www.the-kennel-club.org.uk. This is a great opportunity to develop the bond between dog and owner. You'll both benefit!

Earning a Good Citizen award isn't hard, but it does take preparation and training. Training for the awards is training for good manners and responsible behaviour as well as basic skills every performance dog should know.

Training for the CGC

Many local dog clubs offer classes that specifically prepare you and your dog for the Good Citizen award. For more information on where to find training classes and test evaluators in your state, search the KC web site.

Good Citizen awards are designed to measure just how well-behaved and well-mannered your dog is. You will need a regular buckle collar and lead for the test, but you may not use head halters, harnesses, pinch collars, or any other kind of collars or leads. Most of the exercises are performed with your Golden on the lead. You will also need your dog's regular brush or comb. You may not use any treats or toys as incentive during the test.

If your dog doesn't pass a test, he can take it again on another occasion. A dog will not pass a test if he doesn't complete any of the exercises, or if he growls, snaps, lunges, or bites at the tester or anyone else who is helping in the test.

The exercises become progressively more difficult as you work through bronze, silver and gold levels. The preliminary exercises are very straightforward and include the following:

1. Accepting a friendly stranger
2. Sitting politely for petting
3. Appearance and grooming
4. Out for a walk (walking on a loose lead)
5. Walking through a crowd
6. Sit and down on command and staying in place
7. Coming when called
8. Reaction to another dog
9. Reaction to distraction
10. Supervised separation

And that's it! Do you think your Golden Retriever could pass these steps? If not (yet), start training for this test as a goal. Practice each step until your Golden Retriever is comfortable doing them all. It feels great to earn a Good Citizen award, and you can take pride in knowing that you have a canine good citizen as part of your family.

COMPETITIVE OBEDIENCE

Golden Retrievers are naturals at competitive obedience. This organised event tests dogs on their ability to follow basic instructions. Many clubs hold obedience trials. The Kennel Club and the American Kennel Club both sanction obedience competitions, which are often held as stand-alone events for all breeds or for particular breeds.

Competitive obedience tests dogs on their ability to follow basic instructions.

At the basic or beginners level of competitive obedience, dogs have to demonstrate for a judge that they can do the following:

- Heel on the lead and in a pattern set by the judge, which includes left turns, right turns and about turns
- Heel off the lead in the same pattern as on the lead
- Stand for examination by the judge
- Recall, or reliably coming when called
- Long sit, holding a sit position for one minute
- Long down, holding a down position for two minutes

At more advanced levels, dogs have to do more complicated exercises, which include:

- Retrieves
- Distance control
- Scentwork
- Sendaway

Chaining

Training complicated tricks isn't all that complicated, if you break the tricks down into steps, a training method called chaining. For example, if you want your Golden Retriever to turn off the light switch, you can train him to touch a piece of tape by luring him to it with some food and giving him a treat when he touches it with his nose. As he does this, say "touch." Practice this again and again, until your dog does it reliably. Then, you can start to move the tape across the floor, up the wall, and onto a light switch.

Do each part a little at a time, making each link in the chain solid before moving to the next step. This also works for training dog sports like agility. Teach each piece of this obstacle course individually, practicing over and over until your Golden understands it. Then, move on to the next step. This keeps training manageable and lets your Golden Retriever succeed over and over. With Golden Retrievers, frequent success is a much better motivator than frequent failure.

At the higher levels, the heelwork becomes increasingly complicated, and must be conducted at a variety of paces—fast, normal and slow. The stay exercise is conducted with the handler out of sight.

The greatest honour in obedience competition is for the dog to be made an Obedience Champion. This happens when a dog, competing in the highest class, wins three separate Challenge Certificates from three different judges.

RALLY

Rally is a new sport that some people call "obedience light." It is not currently available in the UK, but it is proving so popular in the US that it will not be long before it finds its way over here. It is a fun, low-pressure form of competitive obedience in which dogs compete to earn titles. The dog and the handler move through a series of stations that the Rally judge has set up, following the instructions for the task to be performed at each station. Many people see Rally as the perfect next step for a dog and owner who have earned the Good Citizen award but aren't yet quite ready for competitive obedience…or just don't want to compete in that kind of environment.

Rally has classes or levels like obedience, but different titles:

- In the Novice class, dogs can earn the Rally Novice (RN) title.
- In the Advanced class, dogs can win the Rally Advanced (RA) title.
- In the Excellent class, dogs can win the Rally Excellent (RE) title.
- In the Advanced Excellent class, dogs can win the Rally Advanced Excellent (RAE) title.

CANINE FREESTYLE

Also called Heelwork to Music (HTM), this fun riff on formalised obedience allows handlers to choreograph "dances" between handler and dog using obedience moves and other tricks set to music. Performances are fun and amazing to watch, and include costumes. The dances dogs and handlers invent and perform together are truly amazing.

IN THE FIELD

Let's not forget the Golden Retriever's original function, as a hunting companion. Many Golden Retrievers retain a strong

Your Golden Retriever can excel at organised field activities.

instinct to hunt and retrieve, and watching a Golden Retriever's instinct kick in during a field trial, or a casual weekend hunting expedition is truly a thing of beauty. Of course, most Golden Retriever owners don't hunt with their pets, and some of them wouldn't be interested in field trials, hunt tests, or even tracking. However, if you want to see your Golden Retriever fulfilling his original purpose and you enjoy the outdoors, you might look into activities in the field.

Field Trials

In UK field trials nothing is staged or artificial. A handler will not know in advance what type of game his dog will be expected to retrieve, or what type of terrain the dog will have to work in—it could be swamp, woodland or undergrowth. If a dog flushes unshot game when he is sent out to retrieve, he must ignore it.

In a walked up field trial, gundogs are expected to walk in a line that may include 6 dogs, 3-4 judges, 6-8 guns, stewards and game carriers. The dogs are off lead. A dog can go out to retrieve only when he is given a command by his handler. Dogs must wait quietly while other dogs are working.

At a drive, the dogs must sit in a line while birds are flushed out by the beaters over the dogs and the guns. The shot or wounded birds will fall, but again a dog must wait for the command to retrieve.

The dogs are judged on their natural game-finding abilities, their response to the handler and on their work in the shooting field. The most valued qualities in a working gundog are steadiness and obedience.

Hunting Tests

In America, field trials reached such a high level that many people, who enjoyed working with their dogs simply as a recreation, were unable to devote the time needed to offer serious competition to the more professional triallists. In response to this, the American Kennel Club introduced hunting competitions.

The competitions are not as "extreme" as field trials (which have been likened to a form of doggie Olympics), but more closely resemble real hunting situations. They employ the same skills as field trials, but take place over less distance. Competitors are not awarded places, as in Field Trials, but those that finish the course are given "completions".

Tracking

Tracking is an organised sport that tests any breed's ability to follow a scent. This is a fun sport for Golden Retrievers, and for people who like to spend a lot of time training outside. In the UK, tracking is incorporated in Working Trials, which is a discipline that also involves control and agility, and in the the advanced stages, manwork (catching and apprehending a "criminal"). Golden Retrievers have proved to be very successful in this challenging sport.

In the US, tracking is a sport in its own right. To start with, dogs are given a scent and must find a glove. They can't just go straight to the glove, but must follow the scent trail as it has been laid out. Dogs experienced at tracking can go on to do other tracking-related work like search and rescue or drug detection.

At the basic level, the scent trail is laid out in an open field and is about 500 yards long with three to five turns in the trail. The trail is aged about two hours. As the levels get tougher, trails get longer with more turns, distracting cross tracks and obstacles like roads, ditches, and woods. They are also aged longer so the scent trail is

Tracking as a Profession

Golden Retrievers who show a particular penchant for tracking are often trained to specialise in search and rescue work, drug detection work, or other police or military work involving that incredible canine nose.

In search and rescue, dogs may be trained to find lost hikers, hunt down criminals, find survivors in a disaster, or help to locate bodies. Many Golden Retrievers worked on the scene of both the World Trade Center disaster in New York City and the Oklahoma City bombing.

Drug detection dogs may work with police officers or at customs, and may also be trained to detect other illegal contraband, or to detect bombs and other explosives. Many states and individual training schools offer search and rescue training programmes, as well as training in police and military work.

Agility is a fun, fast-moving competition that includes jumping over obstacles.

older and fainter. Any breed can compete in tracking, and this sport is a lot of fun. Tracking people are famous for their willingness to help beginners get into the sport, and Golden Retrievers typically enjoy this time outdoors with their people.

Titles in organised tracking events include:

- Tracking Dog (TD)
- Tracking Dog Excellent (TDX)
- Variable Surface Tracker (VST)
- Champion Tracker (CT)

CANINE SPORTS

Does your Golden Retriever just want to have fun? Maybe canine sports are for you. Canine sports have become very popular, because dogs and their owners enjoy them so much! From agility's obstacle courses to competitive dock jumping, canine sports are a great way to keep both you and your Golden Retriever in shape. Here are some of your options:

Agility

Agility is a fun, fast-moving competition in which dogs compete, one at a time, to navigate an obstacle course. The fastest dog and handler wins. The course includes:

- Jumps
- Tunnels

- Weaves
- A-frame
- Dog walk
- See-saw

And don't think the dog does all the work, either. Handlers run alongside their dogs, directing them through the obstacles in the correct order, as specified by the judge. Everybody gets a workout. Agility is almost as fun to watch as it is to do. In fact, it is so popular that many trainers and dog clubs offer special classes just for agility. Dogs can practice the different obstacles and dog-handler teams can practice their teamwork, with the handler directing the dog over the obstacles and timing the run. Even if you never plan to compete, agility classes are fun.

There are two types of class to compete in: Jumping classes, which include jumps, weaves and tunnels, and Agility classes, which have a full set of equipment.

Agility can damage a dog's joints when carried out without adequate supervision, so it is always best to join a club and train with an experienced instructor. Check out the Kennel Club website (www.the-kennel-club.org.uk) for more details.

Flyball

Flyball is an exciting, fast-paced relay race. Dogs compete in teams, usually with four dogs on each team. Invented in California in the 1970s, flyball caught on quickly and soon became a highly competitive international sport.

In a flyball race, the first dog on each team dashes over four hurdles, hits a flyball box that releases a ball, grabs the ball, dashes back over the hurdles, and crosses the finish line, at which point the next dog does the same thing. Whichever team finishes first wins. Individual dogs win points according to team wins.

Flyball is dominated by fast Border Collies—a breed well known for their love of tennis balls. Goldens can do well in this sport, but to be successful, your Golden must be ball-mad. You can start playing with a tennis ball and your Golden will soon see this as his favourite treat. Build up your dog's enthusiasm and motivation by supervising all games with the tennis ball rather than allowing the dog free access. You will also need to work on a really strong recall, so that your Golden will come racing back to you with the ball in his mouth, despite the distractions of other dogs and spectators.

You can teach your Golden to retrieve Frisbees.

Frisbee/Disc Dog

Canine disc is a recognised sport in the US. At the present time, we have demonstrations of canine disc in he UK, but it is not yet an organised sport and has still to be recognised the Kennel Club.

At the most basic level, the handler throws a disc from a designated area, and the dog has to run after it and catch it in the air, before it hits the ground. With each successive level, the distance the dog has to run grows, and other requirements are added, such as requiring that a certain number of catches be completed within a certain amount of time or within a certain number of throws.

Many Goldens take to therapy work intuitively.

Dock Jumping

This all-American sport is the ultimate for Goldens who love to swim and love to retrieve—and most Goldens love both. A new sport, dock jumping is fun and competitive. Dog-handler teams take turns going to the end of a dock. The handler throws a "Chase object" into the water and the dog jumps after it. Jumps are digitally measured by the judges using special equipment. Dogs with the longest jumps win.

Many Goldens take to this sport naturally, but you may need to train them to jump as far as possible rather than jumping in a short distance and swimming the rest of the way.

THERAPY WORK

Therapy dogs work in hospitals and nursing homes visiting people. Many pet owners do therapy work with their dogs, and many dogs take to this job intuitively, knowing exactly which people seem to need a friendly golden coat to pet and which ones would rather be left alone. Training to be a therapy dog is more complicated than knowing how to stand nicely for petting. Hospitals and nursing homes have liability issues, and they can't risk a patient being bitten or injured when a dog jumps on them.

In the UK, an organisation called Pets as Therapy tests dogs for their suitability for therapy work. If your dog is successful, you can become an accredited representative.

The stories people tell about therapy work with dogs are pretty amazing. Nursing home residents who were completely unresponsive suddenly seem to wake up and smile when a dog comes into the room and nuzzles up to them. People with terminal illness, including children, eagerly await a favourite dog's weekly visit. Some dogs will pull people in wheelchairs down the hallway, or just sit on a bed and offer a listening ear. For many people who had dogs long ago, the sudden presence of a dog can be comforting and invigorating. Therapy dogs truly work miracles.

Safety Tips for Canine Athletes

Sports are a great way to stay in shape for both dogs and humans, but they also come with a certain risk of injury—for both dogs and humans. When competing in performance events with your Golden athlete, take the following precautions:

- Avoid high-impact activity until puppies are full grown. Sports like agility and flyball involve jumping, and this kind of high-impact activity isn't good for large breed puppies. Too much stress from high-impact activities could impede correct, healthy joint development, causing orthopaedic problems later in life. You can introduce puppies to agility and flyball equipment, but don't have them jump through hoops or over hurdles until they have finished growing, at about one year of age.
- Just like humans, dogs have to warm up and cool down before and after strenuous exercise. A brisk walk should do the trick. Without a warmup or cooldown, your dog risks injuring himself. A stretched tendon or a torn muscle can be very painful and could signal the end of your dog's competitive days.
- If your Golden Retriever is out of shape, don't launch him immediately into strenuous activity. He needs to get back into condition gradually. High-level performance events are for canine athletes in peak condition, not for "armchair" Goldens. Train your dog sensibly, with moderate increases in activity as his fitness level increases.
- If your dog falls and is injured, see a veterinary surgeon to be sure there are no broken bones, and to get a proper treatment protocol. You may find the services of a physiotherapist who specialises in treating dogs is useful.
- Always be aware of other dogs at performance events. While any competing dog should be trustworthy around other dogs, sometimes an aggressive dog shows up at an event.

At Your Service

Golden Retrievers are one of the most popular breeds to use as assistance dogs. Types of assistance work can include guiding the visually impaired, hearing dogs, assistance dogs for the mobility impaired, and seizure alert dogs. Training varies according to what the dog will be doing, but often, puppies are raised by puppy socialisers working with training programmes in these areas. When they are ready to graduate to the training programme, they go through the screening process and training to see if they can qualify to work as an assistance dog. Those who do not qualify, for a variety of reasons (energy level, personality, etc.), are placed in pet homes, sometimes with the original person who raised the puppy.

Those who do qualify are placed with a new owner, as an assistance dog. This is a rewarding role for Golden Retrievers and makes a huge impact on the lives of those who need assistance: it is a truly mutual partnership between dog and human. For more information on these programmes contact the individual charities: Guide Dogs for the Blind Association, Dogs for the Disabled, Canine Partners, and Hearing Dogs.

The great thing about therapy work is how rewarding it is to watch. Owners often claim they do virtually nothing, they just step back and let their dogs visit the people they know need them. Golden Retrievers are such a popular and beloved breed that they make great therapy dogs. Many people recognise them and remember other Golden Retrievers they have known. Older Goldens with calm temperaments make the best choices, but every individual therapy dog has his own strengths, and plenty of younger Goldens have made a big impact in therapy.

SHOWING YOUR DOG (CONFORMATION)

Everybody thinks their Golden Retrievers are beautiful, and many pet owners entertain the thought of trotting their Golden Retrievers around a dog show ring. "My Golden Retriever is way prettier than the dog that won that dog show," you might snicker in front of the TV. But does your Golden Retriever really have what it takes to compete in the show ring?

Subjective visions of Golden beauty aren't relevant when it comes to the conformation ring. While people often liken dog shows to beauty contests, the whole purpose of a dog show is to evaluate breeding stock. While you might find "fun matches" with less strict rules, the dog show in its classic form judges unneutered and unspayed dogs according to how closely they match the written breed standard—a description of the ideal for any given breed. A neutered pet won't qualify. Nor will a Golden Retriever who is over the height limit, or who has an underbite or overbite. Breed standards specifically evaluate breeding stock according to that dog's ability to perform the function for which he was originally intended. For Golden Retrievers, that means they must be built properly and healthy enough to last for hours in the field to retrieve fallen game willingly, to withstand harsh weather, and to stay close by their owners, waiting for direction. They also have to get along well with other dogs who might be in the hunting pack. Obviously, all of this involves an evaluation of temperament as well as structure. Goldens have to be well built, in good condition, and with a proper coat, but they also have to exhibit the proper friendly, attentive, and biddable nature so important in a good sporting dog.

For Kennel Club-sanctioned shows, dogs must be registered with the KC, be six months of age or older, and be a breed recognised in that particular show. Some shows are all-breed shows, which have different judging rings throughout the day or weekend to judge all recognised breeds. Some are group shows. In the case of the Golden Retriever, these would be Gun Dog shows that recognise all the retrievers, pointers, spaniels, and other sporting breeds. Also, many dog clubs have breed shows. For instance, a local Golden Retriever club might hold a show where only Goldens may compete.

Dogs who are competitive in dog shows must closely meet the official written breed standard. Judges study the Golden Retriever standard and use it to judge Golden Retrievers according to which one most closely fits the written description of Golden Retriever perfection. Judges penalise deviations from the breed standard according to their severity. They pet and feel the dog to be sure he is built correctly. They examine the head shape and set of the ears, the eye and muzzle shape, the set of the tail, the shape of the feet, the shape of the body, the condition and quality of the coat, the colour, and the way the Golden Retriever moves. And of course, any Golden Retriever who appears shy or aggressive or uncooperative will not be winning any ribbons.

Your Golden Retriever might well be the best pet you ever had, and in your eyes, flawless. If you aren't breeding your Golden Retriever, faults don't matter. But if your Golden Retriever does closely match the breed standard, if you have officially registered your Golden Retriever with the Kennel

What to Wear to Show a Dog

Dog shows are formal events. You won't see jeans and T-shirts out there in the ring. Dogs are supposed to look their best, and so should the handler. However, the handler should not dress to distract from the dog, but to complement the dog. Conservative is better. Most men wear suits and women wear dresses or jackets and skirts with flats (you have to run with your dog). Choose a colour that will best set off your Golden Retriever's coat. Typically, the bigger the dog show, the more formal the dress.

The dog show in its classic form judges dogs according to how closely they match the written breed standard.

Club (or another organisation that sanctions dog shows, like the American Kennel Club, or the United Kennel Club), and if your dog is not spayed or castrated, you could show your dog in dog shows.

Showing your dog is a lot of fun, not only because it is a great activity to do with your dog, but because you get to spend time seeing a lot of other beautiful dogs, and learning about what exactly makes dogs "correct" according to their breed standards. Some dogs thrive on the attention of the crowd and really ham it up. The best dogs win the title of Champion, and this title is then listed before the dog's name, such as Ch. Merriweather's Thunderous Applause (even if you call him "Thunder").

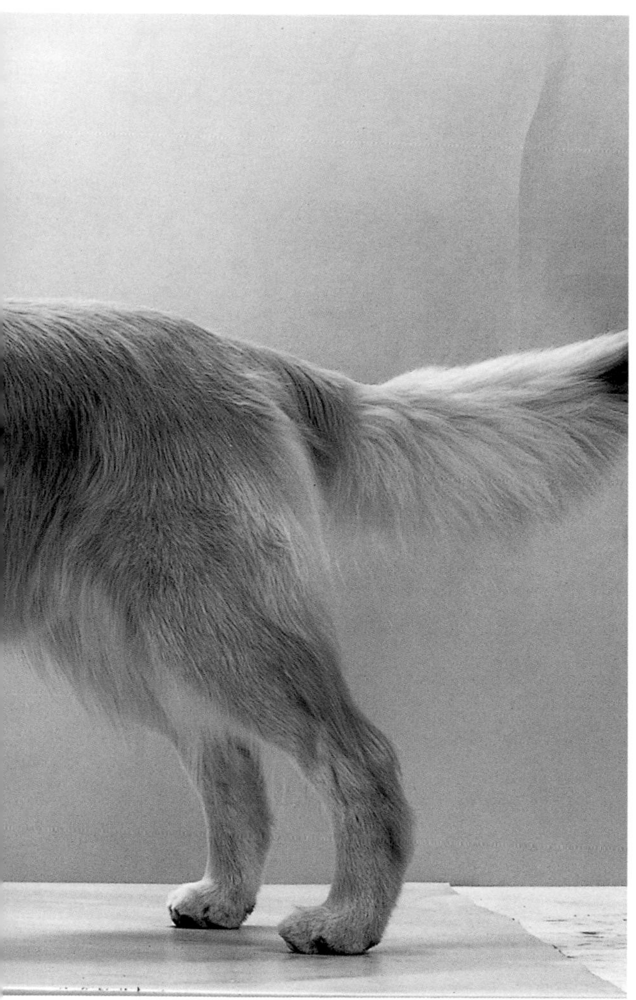

How Dog Shows Work

Dog shows can seem pretty complicated when you first attend one and try to work out what is going on, even as a spectator. But this is a highly organised sport. Dogs are trying to earn that coveted title of champion, and to do this, a dog must earn three Challenge Certificates under three different judges. Challenge Certificates are on offer only at Championship shows, and in these competitions the best male and female will be awarded a CC.

In a dog show, dogs are individually exhibited by their handlers. This can be the pet owner, the breeder, or a professional handler. In the US, professional handlers are used in high-profile dog shows, but in the UK most Goldens are handled by their owners. Handlers bring the dogs out into the ring and the judge examines each one, and also watches all the dogs move around the ring together. Typically, the judge eliminates all but a handful at first, then even more carefully studies the finalists.

At the first level, dogs are divided into classes, and in each class, males and females are judged separately. Rosettes will be awarded to dogs in the highest places. When the judge has

Winners What?

Yes, Winners Bitch. People new to the world of dog shows tend to giggle about this at first, but technically, a "dog" is a male canine and a "bitch" is a female canine. The more experience you have with dog shows, the more "bitch" becomes just another word, as in, "She is an all-around gorgeous bitch." In the dog world, nobody thinks that is a strange thing to say.

Kennel Club Sporting Events

The Kennel Club in the United Kingdom sponsors a variety of events for dogs and their owners to enjoy together. For complete listings, rules, and descriptions, please refer to the Kennel Club's web site at www.the-kennel-club.org.uk.

Agility

Introduced in 1978 at Crufts, agility is a fun, fast-paced, and interactive sport. The event mainly consists of multiple obstacles on a timed course that a dog must handle. Different classes have varying levels of difficulty.

Flyball

Flyball is an exciting sport introduced at Crufts in 1990. Competition involves a relay race in which several teams compete against each other and the clock. Equipment includes hurdles, a flyball box, backstop board, and balls.

Obedience

Obedience competitions test owner and dog's ability to work together as a team. There are three types of obedience tests, which include the Limited Obedience Show, Open Obedience Show, and Championship Obedience Show. Competition becomes successively more difficult with each type of show.

Field Trials

Field trials are designed to test a gundog's ability to work in his natural environment and under competitive conditions. These trials are very similar to a day of hunting in the field, and a variety of game is used.

Gundog Working Tests (GWTs)

Gundog Working Tests are designed to test a dog's natural working ability while promoting sound gundog work. There are three different types of Gundog Working Tests, and each is designed for different breeds of dog.

Working Trials

The first working trial took place in 1924 and was held by the Associated Sheep, Police, and Army Dog Society. Working trials test a dog's working ability and include five levels of competition known as stakes. Each stake is made up of exercises in control, agility, and nosework.

finished judging all the classes, it is time to find the overall winners.

The judge must look at his class winners and select the best male and the best female. This is no easy task, as he will be evaluating dogs of different ages, from puppies of a mere six months of age, right up to advanced, experienced show dogs. A number of dogs may already be Champions, so it is a very tough challenge for young, upcoming dogs to come forward.

The judge will make his choice and will select his winning male and female. If Challenge Certificates are on offer, both dogs will be awarded a CC. However, there is one final honour the breed judge can award—and that is Best of Breed. The judge will make a thorough evaluation of each dog, and will then declare a Best of Breed.

In a breed show, the Best of Breed winner is equivalent to winning Best in Show. But in an all-breed show, the Best of Breed (BOB) still has a way to go. The next step is to compete in the Group ring. For Golden Retrievers, that means your winning BOB Golden goes into the ring with all the other Gundog breeds. (What this group is called depends on the organisation sanctioning the show. The Kennel Club (Britain's national registry) and the UKC in America call this group the Gundog group, while the AKC (America's main national registry) calls this group the Sporting group.

That means the best Golden Retriever will compete against the best Labrador Retriever, Chesapeake Bay Retriever, and all the other retrievers, as well as all the other pointers, setters, spaniels, and other sporting or gun dogs like the Weimaraner and the Vizsla. People wonder how a judge can choose between different breeds like a Golden Retriever and, for example, a Wirehaired Pointing Griffon, but the dogs aren't really being judged against each other. They are each being evaluated according to how well each dog meets his own breed standard. This is a tough job for a judge because they have to be well acquainted with all the standards and be able to decide which dog best meets his own standard.

The best gundog will then be awarded Best of Group. Meanwhile, in other rings, each Best of Breed in every other category is competing for their own Best of Gundog Group, so that at the end of this level of competition, dogs have been whittled down to seven: the Best of Group in each of the seven breed groups: Sporting, Hound, Working, Terrier, Toy, Utility, and Pastoral.

But the fun isn't over yet! The ultimate honour in a dog show is to win Best in Show, and in a large all-breed dog show, this is quite an accomplishment. The seven Best in Group finalists enter the ring, and a Best in Show judge has the difficult task of choosing which among them—from Chihuahua to Newfoundland—best meets its individual breed standard. One dog is awarded Best in Show (BIS). Breeders consider the

Probably the very best way to learn about dog shows is to attend them as a spectator.

number of BIS titles won in a dog's career a serious indicator of quality for breeding stock, and indeed it is. Because remember, that is the original point of this whole complicated event. A Golden Retriever puppy with multiple BIS parents is probably going to be an excellent example of a Golden Retriever, as it is meant to be.

Dog Shows for Beginners

Doesn't that all sound like a lot of fun? It really is, but it is also a highly competitive pursuit. If that sounds like your kind of thing, check out the Kennel Club's web site for more information on participating in dog shows, and talk to your breeder. Many dog clubs also offer ringcraft classes, to teach you the ropes before you ever enter the ring. They can also offer good support and practice after you have started to show, and can introduce you to other people in your area who show their dogs.

Before you show your dog, be sure that your dog's KC, AKC, or UKC registration is in order. Dogs must not be spayed or castrated and must be current on their vaccinations. Dogs in the show ring should be well groomed, but Golden Retrievers don't require a lot. Brush his coat, trim stray hairs, trim feet to be nice and neat, make sure nails are clipped, and go! Some people also trim the Golden's whiskers, for a neater muzzle.

Probably the very best way to learn about dog shows is to attend them as a spectator before ever showing your dog. Conformations are complicated but the more you experience them, the easier it gets. Look for benched shows near you. Every year Crufts is given extensive television coverage, and this can be a useful guide.

Look over the rules for conformation shows before entering, so you have an idea of what is going on, and practice, practice, practice. Dogs must follow you (on a lead) and stand nicely for the judge. They must also allow the judge to examine them, and naturally they should be well behaved and under control, so

Benched Shows

Some dog shows are called benched shows. That means that, when they are not competing, dogs and their handlers (and often their breeders and owners) hang out in a benching area, with the dogs resting in their kennels, where spectators can go and visit the dogs. This is a great opportunity for people new to dog shows or interested in different breeds to look at different dogs and ask questions of the breeders and handlers. You might find the perfect breeder for your new puppy in the benching area. Or, get answers to your questions about dog shows. Many people are very willing to talk to you, but use common sense, too. If a handler and a dog are just getting ready to go into the ring, they are both probably a little nervous, or at least getting mentally prepared. Wait until they are done to talk to them.

A successful show dog must be well behaved and enjoy working in front of a crowd.

that they don't chase other dogs or jump on anybody. Get those requirements down, and go for it! You might find a whole new hobby that brings fun and excitement to you and your Golden Retriever.

Chapter 8

HEALTH of Your Golden Retriever

Golden Retriever puppies may be the picture of glowing health, with their shiny, soft coats, moist dark eyes, and energetic wiggling bodies. Like human children, however, dogs need regular preventive care, attention, good nutrition, vaccinations, a healthy lifestyle, a good health care provider, and a guardian prepared for emergencies. Keeping your Golden healthy, and even addressing health problems that do arise, will be much easier with the right knowledge and preparation.

Most Golden Retrievers live healthy lives, but this breed is prone to certain genetic problems. If you buy your Golden Retriever puppy from a good breeder who is working to eliminate health defects from the breed, you have a better chance of having a pet who will live a long, healthy, disease-free life. Yet, even the best bred dogs can eventually develop diseases, structural problems like hip dysplasia, and some of the diseases that ageing humans often develop, like heart disease and cancer. Goldens can also suffer from accidents—a cut, a broken bone, poisoning. Nobody likes to think about their dog having any of these problems, but the prepared pet owner can deal with these problems quickly, catch them early, and have them treated appropriately. That gives everybody the best chance for a happy ending.

A GOOD VET IS GOLDEN

One of the very first things to do when you first bring home your new puppy or adopted older Golden Retriever is see a veterinary surgeon. Some breeders require this as part of their contract and health guarantee, and many rescue centres also strongly encourage a vet check at the very beginning of your life with your new dog. This initial vet visit allows your vet to check your new puppy or dog for signs of disease or other problems, but it is also the first time your vet and your new dog will meet. It may be the first time you meet the vet, too. Is this the vet for you?

Every dog needs a vet, not just for times of illness and injury but for regular health checks, disease prevention, and as a source of good advice. Vets have seen a lot, and they can advise you about a good food, whether or not to use supplements, how to prevent parasites, and even, in some cases, behaviour and training issues and holistic health approaches.

But not all vets feel the same way about every brand of pet food, supplement, parasite control method, holistic health therapy, or behaviour and training issues. If you have a preference for more natural treatments, for example, and your vet doesn't, you could soon be at odds with your approach to your Golden's health plan. That's why every new dog owner can benefit from shopping around for a vet. Here are some things to consider.

What Kind of Vet Do You Want?

More than ever before in the history of pets, the veterinary profession has evolved into a wide array of specialties and subspecialties as well as philosophical inclinations. Some vets in rural areas specialise in farm animal care. Some limit their practice to dogs and cats (or just dogs, or just cats). Some have a preference for certain breeds of dogs, or limited experience with rare breeds. Some vets are distinctly holistic in their approach and are likely to

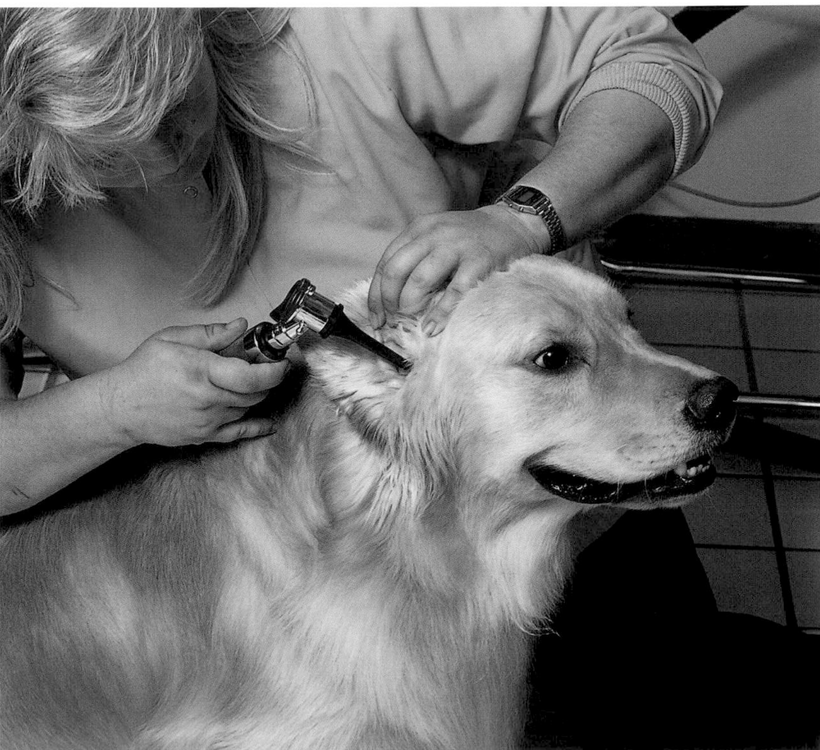

Find a good, experienced vet for your Golden puppy or adult.

suggest homeopathy, acupuncture, or herbal therapy before more conventional approaches.

Today, many vets specialise in very specific areas. Veterinary schools and hospitals all over the country teach and employ veterinary orthopaedic surgeons, veterinary ophthalmologists, veterinary oncologists, veterinary cardiologists, and specialists in a host of other fields. If your dog gets cancer, or glaucoma, or hip dysplasia, or is born with a heart defect, you have the option to get highly advanced care.

For your Golden puppy, however, the first step is to find a good, experienced general vet. How do you know which one is for you?

Probably the best way to find a good vet is via recommendations. Talk to your Golden Retriever's breeder. Talk to your dog-owning friends. Talk to people at dog shows, in pet stores, and at dog parks. Luckily, most vets have a lot of experience with Golden Retrievers because the breed is so popular, but that doesn't mean every vet likes Goldens, or that you will like every vet you meet. You might not even like the vet your friends like or your breeder recommends, but it's a good place to start. Choose a vet with a good reputation, good recommendations, and experience.

Then, schedule an appointment, either for an interview (expect to pay for a visit to the surgery), or for a check-up for your dog. Once you arrive, pay attention to your surroundings. How are you treated at the surgery? Are the staff friendly? Do you have to wait a long time, or less than 15 minutes? Does the vet spend relaxed time with you finding out about your dog, interacting with your dog, and allowing you to ask questions? Or, do you feel rushed or as if you are imposing on your vet's busy schedule?

Also consider how your vet and your dog react to each other. Many dogs are nervous and agitated or even fearful at a veterinary surgery. Does the vet put your dog at ease? Do you like the way your vet talks to and handles your dog? Or do you feel like the vet doesn't really appreciate your pet? You should have a good feeling about your vet, and assuming your vet is well qualified and comes with good recommendations, this is an important consideration.

The feeling you get about your vet and the testimonials from others mean a lot, but don't forget practical considerations, either. When choosing a vet, think about location and price, too. How fast can you get to a veterinary

practice if something should happen and your dog needs treatment quickly? If you love the vet with the surgery far away, is there a practice nearer to you, just in case? If your dog has a health problem and has to visit the vet frequently, how far do you want to drive? Is the vet accessible in inclement weather?

Price probably shouldn't be your only consideration, but it can be a factor. Call several different vets in your area and ask about prices for basic services like office visits, annual check-ups, vaccinations, and worming treatment. You may find quite a difference from vet to vet. Some vets charge a lot more than others, and in some cases, this is due to advanced equipment and training, but in other cases, it may simply be because the vet is more conveniently located. Many people prefer to drive farther for a vet with more reasonable prices and a better bedside manner. Others don't mind a brusque approach and a higher price tag if it means the latest in veterinary technological advancements. It's really a personal preference.

Questions to Ask Your Vet

Whether you first meet your vet through a scheduled interview or via your first veterinary appointment, you can use that meeting to evaluate the vet, and to help you decide whether this is the vet for you. Your vet should be willing to talk with you about his or her experience, qualifications, and philosophy. Here are some questions to ask:

Preparing Your Golden Retriever for the Vet

Some Goldens bounce happily in the car no matter where you are going, and few show the fear and timidity of some breeds when visiting the vet, but some Goldens, especially young puppies, those with uncertain histories, and those who have had unpleasant vet visits in the past, can react badly to a vet visit. This in itself isn't a sign that you have found the wrong vet. Preparing your Golden for a veterinary visit is the best way to minimise the stress. Try these strategies and your Golden puppy may never learn to fear a visit to the vet:

- Before you take your Golden for a check-up to the vet (even the day before), pay a visit to the vet with your dog. Bring treats and ask the staff to give your dog a treat. The visit should be brief, cheerful, and rewarding.
- Every time you groom your dog, handle him like the vet will handle him. Pick up his paws, touch his nails, look in his ears and eyes, feel along his ribs and abdomen, and look at his teeth. When this becomes a part of the normal grooming routine, your dog won't be surprised when your vet does these same things to him.
- When you visit for a check-up, keep your dog on a lead to minimise unpleasant contact with other animals in the waiting room, and so that you can keep control of your dog. Even if he is well-behaved off-lead at home, you never know what could happen at a vet's surgery with other animals around, especially those that might not appreciate your Golden's friendly overtures.
- Keep records of your dog's behaviour, habits, medications, diet, and symptoms. A daily health journal can provide your vet with specific, invaluable information when he or she is diagnosing a health problem.

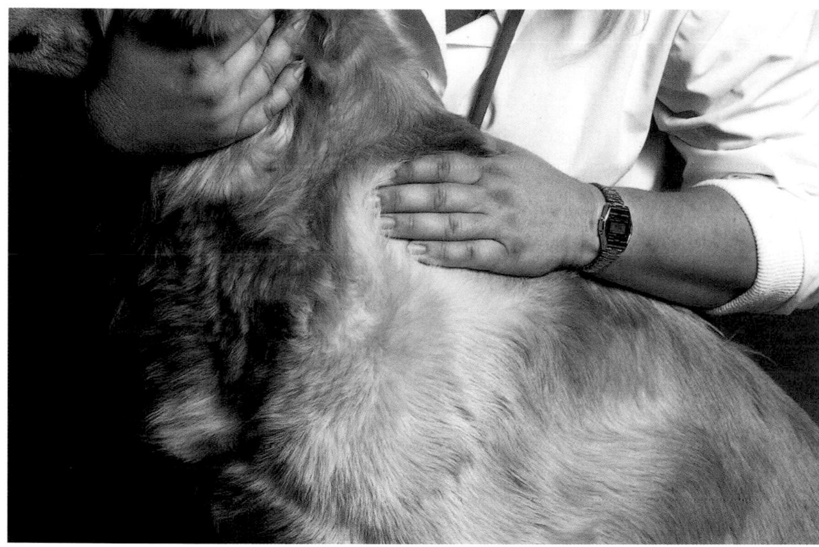

Every time you groom your dog, handle him like the vet will handle him.

- How long have you been a practicing vet?
- Where did you get your degree?
- What is your specialty?
- What made you want to become a vet?
- What do you think about holistic health care?
- How do you feel about Golden Retrievers? Have you treated many of them?
- What are some of the health issues you have seen in Goldens?
- Are there things you recommend I do to keep my dog healthy?

These questions will help to open up a dialogue between you and your vet, and help you to get a sense about how you feel about this person who will be so instrumental in the health care of your Golden. If you don't like the way you and your vet communicate, or your vet's approach to health care, or if you don't like the way the vet handles your dog, you have the right to search for another vet.

WHAT HAPPENS AT THE VET

Puppy's First Check-up

When you bring your Golden Retriever to that very first vet visit, what happens depends to some degree on the vet, but in most cases, you can count on a few standard things. First, be sure you do your part. Bring these things to your puppy's first examination:

- All records of vaccinations and other medical procedures performed previously on the puppy. Get these from the breeder or rescue centre, if available.

- Any written instructions from the breeder or rescue centre.
- Find out if you need to bring a sample of your puppy's stool. The vet can use this stool sample to test for internal worms.
- A list of questions you have, which could include what to feed your dog, questions about Goldens as a breed, behaviour questions, and questions regarding the best ways to keep your dog healthy.

First, your vet will probably conduct a physical examination on your dog, examining his eyes, ears, teeth, body, feet, and rear. The vet can tell a lot of things by poking and prodding, and listening to your dog's heart: skeletal abnormalities, swollen lymph nodes, signs of infection, the condition of your dog's heart, to name just a few. The vet may do a urine and stool test, and possibly a blood test, to have baseline information about your dog and to look for any signs of disease. Your vet might give your new puppy worming medication, and probably a set of vaccinations. You should have a chance to ask questions, and the vet should have a chance to tell you about what he or she perceives to be your Golden Retriever's apparent state of health.

After that, your vet should give you an idea of how often to bring your dog in for a visit. In the case of a healthy dog, an annual examination is the standard, although in the first year, your dog will probably return to the vet more often to receive vaccinations.

Annual Check-ups

The annual examination is an important part of preventive health care for your Golden Retriever. It is your yearly "check-in" with the vet, the time when you can voice concerns about your Golden, ask questions, and monitor how your Golden is growing, changing, and ageing. This is also a chance for your Golden to

Vaccines of the Future

Vaccinations work on the principle that a killed or inactivated virus, or a modified (weakened) virus, introduced into the body, will prompt the immune system to develop immunity against that disease without the body actually developing the disease. This works, but comes with an inherent risk. In some animals, the modified or killed virus could prompt a reaction or, in a few cases, even result in contracting the disease. Scientists have been working on genetically engineered vaccinations that prompt the body to develop an immune response without the risk of a reaction that can sometimes happen when a modified live or inactivated killed virus is introduced into the system. These recombinant vaccines are safer than live vaccines and more effective than killed or inactivated vaccines, and may soon be the norm for vaccinations against many diseases in both animals and humans.

receive any necessary "booster" immunisations, have any necessary on-going health tests, and to buy medications like flea control and worming treatments.

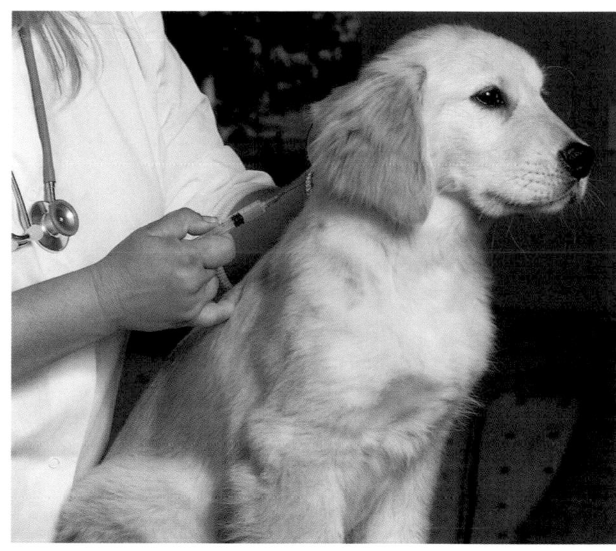

In the first year, vaccinations are an important part of your Golden Retriever's care.

Vaccinations

In the first year, vaccinations are an important part of your Golden Retriever's health care. Vaccinations can almost completely eliminate the chances of your Golden Retriever developing a serious or fatal disease, such as parvovirus or distemper. The DHPP vaccination combination typically protects against distemper, hepatitis, parainfluenza, and parvovirus. Additionally, dogs living in certain countries must get a rabies vaccination at about three months of age, and depending on the dog's risk factor and location, vets may recommend vaccination against leptospirosis, canine coronavirus, and Lyme disease.

These diseases are serious and in many cases, life-threatening. Vaccinations have largely eliminated them from the population, but unvaccinated dogs are still at risk. But there is another side to vaccinations. Not all dogs react well to vaccinations. A very small percentage could contract a disease even after vaccination. More common is a reaction to the vaccines. Sometimes, dogs have a skin reaction, and sometimes they have a serious systemic reaction, such as anaphylactic shock. While these things sound scary and are known risks of vaccinations, most vets agree that the benefits far outweigh the risks and recommend vaccinating puppies anyway, usually according to a schedule similar to the one in the chart, below.

Another recent area of study has been examining how long individual vaccinations actually last. Some vets support vaccinations, but believe they are given too frequently. Studies suggest that some vaccinations, such as the parainfluenza, bordatella, and leptospirosis vaccines, don't last a full year in most dogs, and those at risk (such as show dogs, or dogs living in areas where these diseases are common) should be vaccinated twice yearly. Other vaccinations, such as parvo may last as long as three years in many dogs. Studies also show that vaccinations last longer

Typical Vaccination Schedule for Your Golden Retriever's First Year

Vaccination administration marked by an X, or as noted. This chart is just a guidelinc. Follow your vet's recommendation.

	5 to 8 weeks	8 to 12 weeks	14 to 16 weeks	15 to 18 weeks	Booster
Rabies (if required)	—	first shot at 12 weeks	—	first rabies booster	every one to three years, depending on law and type of vaccine
Distemper	X	X	X	first booster	every one to three years
Parainfluenza	X	X	X	first booter	annually, or twice annually for dogs at risk
Hepatitis	—	X	X	first booster	annually
Paravovirus	X	X	X	first booster	every one to three years
Bordatella (optional)	X	X	X	first booster	annually, or twice annually for dogs at risk
Leptospirosis (optional)	X	X	X	first booster	annually, or twice annually for dogs at risk
Canine Corona Virus (optional)	X	X	X	first booster	annually
Lyme Disease (optional)	—	X	X	first booster	annually

in some individual dogs than in others.

How do you know whether your dog's immune response to any given disease is active or in need of a booster shot? A titer test can reveal the answer. Titers measure immune response to different diseases, and many vets believe that titers should determine whether dogs need booster shots, rather than the routine annual administration of a group of vaccines. Titer tests cost money, however, and not everybody wants to spend extra for a test to determine whether or not they will need to spend additional money on a vaccination. For most dogs, annual vaccinations are probably just fine, but some pet owners choose (and many vets support this choice) to vaccinate every two to three years instead. Ask your vet about titer tests, if it seems like a preferable option to you.

Neutering

Maybe you meant to do it, but never got around to it. Maybe you think it is "unnatural." Maybe you empathise a little too closely with your dog. Or, maybe you think your female should have just one litter of cute little Golden puppies, or your male should be able to experience the joys of canine copulation at least a few times before getting "snipped."

Actually, spaying or castrating your Golden Retriever is very important. Breeders, rescue centres, and rescue groups all try to spread the word that getting your pet neutered is smart. Are they right? Should you listen? Can it really hurt to avoid this simple surgery?

Many dedicated dog breeders work to improve Golden Retrievers

Neutering your Golden Retriever is an important and responsible step to take.

by learning as much as they can about genetics and by producing just a few puppies from targeted breedings designed to produce dogs of true Golden Retriever type with great health and temperament. For most people, however, the commitment, knowledge, and expense of breeding dogs is more than they are willing to take on. Considering how many Golden Retrievers are waiting for good homes in rescue centres and rescue groups, if you can't breed Goldens to make the breed better, then it is best not to breed them at all.

Breeding dogs isn't easy, and it certainly isn't profitable if you do it responsibly and ethically. Even expensive puppies usually barely recover the costs involved in a good breeding: genetic tests for the parents, veterinary care for the mother and the puppies, high-quality nutrition, early vaccinations, and time spent caring for the mother, whelping the puppies, and attending constantly to the brand new litter add up to quite a cost of money, time, and emotional commitment. Add to that the tragedies that every dog breeder sometimes has to face—stillborn puppies, emergency Caesarean sections, and other medical emergencies cause both financial hardship and heartache. Ethical breeders also work hard to place puppies in homes where they will be well loved and cared for throughout their entire lives. They screen potential buyers carefully, and agree to take back the puppies at any time during their lives if the owner is ever unable to keep them. Many breeders feel very strongly that if they bring puppies into the world, those puppies are their responsibility for the rest of their lives.

It simply isn't true that dogs must experience procreation to be healthy or fulfilled. Actually, dogs who have never experienced these things don't know what they are missing, and those neutered early often exhibit more desirable behaviours throughout adolescence and adulthood. Sure, some people feel that neutering dogs is "unnatural," but with the severe pet overpopulation problem in the country today, it is an important measure of control. It is also healthier for pets. Both male and female dogs suffer from fewer cancers of the reproductive organs if they are neutered.

The world is filled with Golden Retrievers. Find one for you, but don't feel compelled to make any more, unless you want to launch into a serious hobby with respect and reverence for the lives you are manipulating and creating. Many breeders and rescue centres offer certificates for low-cost neutering, and many veterinary clinics offer reduced prices for this important service, too. Please take advantage of what veterinary medicine has to offer, reduce your pet's chances of developing cancer, save yourself a whole lot of work, and leave dog breeding to the experts. Neuter your Golden Retriever and feel good about doing the right thing.

WHEN TO CALL THE VET… AND WHEN TO WAIT

With proper care, most Golden Retrievers will lead healthy lives.

Beyond the annual visit, sometimes your dog will need to go to the vet. Just like humans, dogs can get sick or injured, and knowing whether or not your Golden's condition warrants a vet visit can mean the difference between a scare with a happy ending or a tragedy. As a general rule, if you notice any physical or behavioural changes in your Golden, call the vet. Lumps on the skin, rashes, limping, changes in appetite or sleep patterns, hair loss, weight loss, weight gain, or anything else that just doesn't seem normal all warrant veterinary guidance. Sometimes, however, a call isn't enough. There may be situations where you need to get to a veterinary surgery and get there fast. If your Golden experiences any of the following, call the vet immediately:

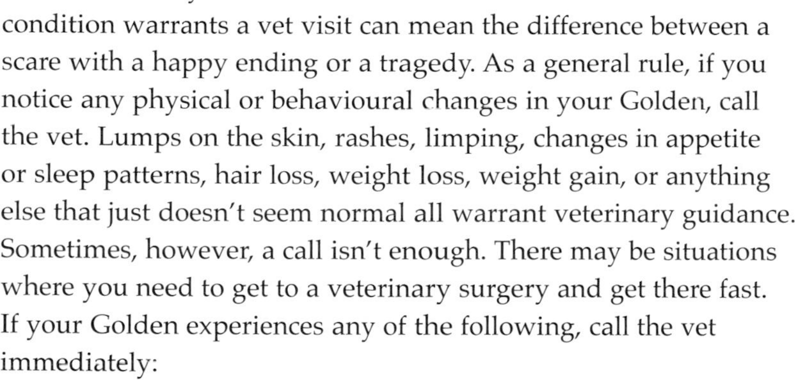

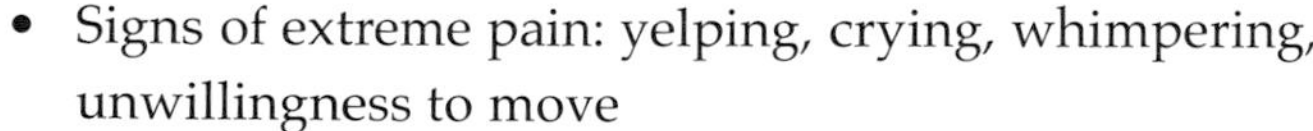

- Signs of extreme pain: yelping, crying, whimpering, unwillingness to move
- Inability to move or to use any limbs
- Sudden laboured breathing
- Collapse, unconsciousness, unresponsiveness
- Seizure
- Bleeding that won't stop after a few minutes or that you can't seem to stop
- Vomiting more than two or three times, especially bloody
- Diarrhoea that lasts for more than one or two days, especially bloody
- Sudden unexplained aggression: growling, biting, attacking for no reason
- If you think your dog ingested any kind of poison
- If your dog was hit by a car (your dog might look fine, but could have internal injuries)

Hip Scoring

In the UK, a hip scoring shceme is run jointly by the Kennel Club and the British Veterinary Association. The average hip scores for every breed are available for checking.

Golden Retriever breeders can have their dogs tested for hip dysplasia, elbow dysplasia and other conditions.

Make sure your Golden's breeder has his breeding stock checked, and ask if you can see the relevant paperwork.

GOLDEN RETRIEVER HEALTH ISSUES

Most Golden Retrievers will lead healthy lives, but every pure breed has certain genetic health issues that they can be prone to developing. In Golden Retrievers, the dominant inheritable diseases are those common to many other breeds, especially of a similar size. The most significant and widespread of these is hip dysplasia, but Goldens are also prone to elbow dysplasia, arthritis, epilepsy, thyroid problems, heart disease, cancer, the bleeding disorder called von Willebrand's disease, and eye problems like cataracts, retinal dysplasia, and progressive retinal atrophy. While most of these conditions are probably genetic, and the chances of your Golden developing them can be reduced by getting your Golden from a breeder specifically working to breed away from serious health problems, any Golden could potentially develop any of these problems. The more you know about these Golden health issues, the better able you will be to detect signs of them and catch them early. In many cases, early treatment is the key to managing these conditions, or even curing them.

Hip Dysplasia

Hip dysplasia is a disease of the hip joint, in which the joint doesn't develop properly and then becomes arthritic with age. Common in large dogs, hip dysplasia is the most prevalent inherited condition in Golden Retrievers, but although it is a genetic disease, it can also be made worse by environment. Goldens already prone to hip dysplasia who grow too quickly (often due to over-nutrition in puppyhood) and/or who stressed their bones too much during growth can develop a severe, crippling case of hip dysplasia, while other Goldens never progress beyond a mild case.

Hip dysplasia can be extremely painful and can debilitate the working dog, sporting dog, or Golden athlete, cutting short a promising career as a field trial dog, agility champion, or assistance dog. Goldens can begin to show signs of hip dysplasia as young as four months, or they may not show any signs until old age. If you notice any of the following in your Golden Retriever, ask your vet to examine your puppy or adult dog for hip dysplasia:

- Limping or rear leg lameness
- A rolling, swaying hip movement when walking or running
- Reluctance or refusal to run, jump, or climb stairs
- Signs of pain with movement or when someone touches the hip

or rear leg area: yelping, crying, even nipping

Unfortunately, there is no cure for hip dysplasia, but in many cases owners can manage hip dysplasia with lifestyle modification. Losing weight or maintaining a slim weight will help to alleviate pain. Nonsteroidal anti-inflammatory drugs often provide great relief, but don't give your Golden a dose of your ibuprofen—make sure to get dosing information appropriate for your dog from your vet. Moderate exercise, therapeutic massage, and hydrotherapy (swimming) can also all make a difference in relieving pain and increasing mobility in dysplastic Goldens. In acute cases of hip dysplasia—extreme lameness and / or chronic pain that isn't helped by other means—your Golden might benefit from surgery. The most common surgeries for hip dysplasia are the triple pelvic osteotomy in young dogs, and femoral head and neck ostectomy or total hip replacement in older dogs. Ask your vet about these options for a severely debilitated Golden.

You can also help to lessen the severity of hip dysplasia in your Golden by doing a few key things in puppyhood:

- Talk to the breeder about hip dysplasia. Responsible Golden

Swimming can help increase mobility if your Golden has a hip problem.

Too much body weight puts additional stress on bones and joints, so keep your Golden's weight under control.

Retriever breeders only breed dogs with sound hips, as certified by a vet via X-ray. The X-rays are then scored, and responsible breeders will breed only with dogs who have a 'good' score. Before you purchase a puppy, you are entitled to see the hip scores of both the sire and the dam. If both parents have good hip scores, your puppy has a lesser chance (although this is still not a complete guarantee) of developing hip dysplasia later in life.

- After the first 12 weeks of life, avoid puppy food, or feed a puppy food for large-breed dogs. These special foods contain lower protein and calcium levels than standard puppy foods, so your Golden grows more slowly. This will allow bones and joints to grow at a rate that will keep them denser and more sound. A premium adult food should be fine for Golden puppies over three months old.
- Don't involve your Golden Retriever puppy in high-impact activities for the first year of life. Agility, running on hard pavement, and any activity that involves vigorous jumping can all compromise joint integrity during this crucial growth stage. Walks and runs on grass are just fine, though. Obviously, your puppy needs exercise, and lots of it.
- Keep your Golden slim. Obesity is the most common affliction in pets, and too much body weight can put additional stress on bones and joints, both during the growth period and as your Golden ages.
- Treat the problem early, to reduce damage from arthritis.

Elbow Dysplasia

Similar to hip dysplasia but afflicting the front legs, elbow dysplasia is a degenerative joint disease of the elbow joints. It isn't as common as hip dysplasia in Golden Retrievers, but about one in ten Golden Retrievers will develop this condition, which usually results in arthritis of the elbow joint in old age.

Like hip dysplasia, elbow dysplasia is probably the result of a combination of genetic and environmental factors, and can be prevented or moderated with the same precautions. Signs usually begin at 5 to 12 months of age, with front leg lameness, stiffness, and pain. In severe cases, elbow surgeries can help, but in most cases, keeping your Golden at a low weight, moderate exercise, and pain medication can lessen the painful symptoms of elbow dysplasia. Breeders should have their dogs tested for elbow dysplasia, using the joint Kennel Club/British Veterinary Association Scheme.

Arthritis

While up to 20 percent of pet dogs have arthritis, some breeds are more at risk than others. Unfortunately, Golden Retrievers have several risk factors that make them even more likely to develop osteoarthritis than some other breeds. First, Golden Retrievers are genetically predisposed to arthritis. Second, joint abnormalities like hip dysplasia and elbow dysplasia are likely to lead to arthritis. Third, working dogs and canine athletes tend to get arthritis from repetitive stress on joints.

Signs of arthritis include:

- Reluctance to exercise, climb stairs, or run
- Yelping when someone touches a painful joint
- Lameness
- Swollen joints
- Crackling sound from the joints, with movement

Osteoarthritis in dogs is similar to the condition in people. The cartilage in joints gets worn down over the years and bones rub together, becoming stiff and painful. Vets diagnose arthritis by performing a physical examination and sometimes doing X-rays to get a closer look at the condition of the joints. They may even

Weight management and moderate exercise can help your arthritic Golden.

In the US, the Golden Retriever Club of America is funding research for the heart disease SAS, in order to resolve this serious genetic problem in Golden Retrievers.

take joint fluid to rule out rheumatoid arthritis or a bacterial or fungal infection, because some diseases like Lyme disease can cause arthritis when bacteria gets inside the joint.

Arthritis is also treated much the same way in dogs and in humans, with nonsteroidal anti-inflammatory medication (sometimes called NSAIDs). But don't give your dog any of your own arthritis medication or any of those ibuprofen pills. Get a prescription in the dosage that is correct for your dog, if he is in pain, and follow your vet's instructions.

You can minimise the effects of arthritis in other ways, too. Some important ways to keep your potentially arthritic dog pain free include:

- Keep your Golden Retriever at a healthy weight. You should be able to feel, but not see, his ribs and he should have a discernible tuck-in at the waist. Excess weight puts extra stress on joints, aggravating arthritis.
- Try natural supplements. Many pet owners and even many scientific studies support the claim that natural supplements with ingredients like glucosamine, chondroitin, and other natural ingredients (but glucosamine in particular) actually improve joint function and offer some relief from arthritis pain and stiffness.
- Exercise moderately. While an arthritic dog doesn't need to be barreling over hurdles to take first place in a flyball race, moderate exercise in the form of daily walks and games of fetch are important for keeping joints mobile and pain-free.
- In severe cases of arthritis, joint replacement surgery can be very helpful with relieving pain and restoring mobility. Lots of Golden Retrievers have had successful hip replacement surgery. Your vet can tell you more about this option.

These tips probably sound familiar if you have arthritis, because they are the same things doctors recommend for arthritic humans. Although arthritis is a common problem in dogs—experts estimate that up to 20 percent of all pet dogs have arthritis—you can usually manage your Golden Retriever's arthritis well enough to keep him relatively free of discomfort.

Heart Disease

In Golden Retrievers, the most common form of heart disease is subvalvular aortic stenosis, or SAS—a condition in which the passageway below the left ventricle is too narrow. Goldens may have no signs of the condition, or they may have an audible heart murmur. SAS can be mild or severe. In severe cases, Goldens can die suddenly, without any warning, and afflicted dogs should never be bred from. Responsible breeders will have their dogs screened by a veterinary cardiologist for signs of SAS. Ask your breeder for information relating to your puppy's parents.

Signs of heart disease in Golden Retrievers may include breathing problems, coughing, inability to exercise for very long, fever, and fainting. Severe cases caught early enough may benefit from medications (beta-blockers), exercise restriction, and periodic chest X-rays and/or echocardiograms. Some vets recommend surgery, although this has not been shown to increase lifespan. If your Golden Retriever has heart disease, seek out a veterinary cardiologist who can best advise you about treatment and managed home care for this all-too-common disease.

Epilepsy

Epilepsy is simply the occurrence of seizures. Many things, including reactions to medications, pesticides, or other toxins, can cause seizures, but in Golden Retrievers epilepsy can be an inherited condition. As with other genetic conditions, afflicted dogs should not be bred from, so before you buy a Golden Retriever puppy, ask the breeder about epilepsy. Unlike hip dysplasia, there isn't an official registry or a score that the breeder can show you to prove the parents are epilepsy free, but a trustworthy breeder will be frank about epilepsy in his or her lines, and would not breed any Goldens with this condition.

Witnessing a seizure in your dog can be a frightening experience, but just imagine how your Golden feels! It is important to stay calm when your dog has a seizure, and to let your vet know about it afterwards. (If the seizure lasts for more than five minutes, call your vet immediately. You may need to go to the surgery.) In most cases, seizures are short-lived episodes of a few seconds to a few minutes. They may be mild—your dog may develop a fixed gaze and become unresponsive for a few minutes—or they can be severe.

In a severe seizure, your Golden may fall over on his side, twitch, shake, salivate, lose bladder control, and paddle his legs. The most important thing to do in this case is to keep your Golden

Stress and Epilepsy

If you are living with an epileptic Golden, try to keep him as stress free as possible. Stress can trigger seizures.

Mention any physical or behavioural changes in your dog to your vet that you can't explain.

safe from hurting himself and from falling. Stay by his side and pet him. Talk reassuringly to him. When the seizure is over, your Golden will probably be confused and may think he did something wrong, especially if he lost bladder control. Talk softly and gently to your Golden until he is recovered. Some dogs take a few minutes to recover, others can take a few days.

If your Golden has congenital (sometimes called idiopathic) epilepsy, he will probably continue to have seizures periodically. Medications can lessen the number and severity of seizures, but probably won't eliminate them altogether. Phenobarbital is the most commonly prescribed seizure medication, but some vets prescribe Valium, diazepam, or drugs containing bromide.

Epilepsy is not a fatal disease, and it isn't painful for your Golden Retriever, but it can be upsetting for everyone involved, especially if the pet owner makes a big deal about it. It is up to you to provide the calm, reassuring care your Golden needs.

Hypothyroidism

This disorder of the endocrine gland usually shows itself by four to seven years of age. Just as with humans, hypothyroidism is difficult to diagnose. Signs include weight gain, loss of energy, depression, cold intolerance, dry skin, thinning coat, constipation or diarrhoea, and many other general symptoms that are also symptoms of lots of other disorders. To diagnose hypothyroidism, your vet will probably do a blood test, urine test, and a number of other tests including a detailed history of symptom development. The good news is that hypothyroidism is easy to treat with a daily dose of synthetic hormone. This usually completely resolves the symptoms and a Golden with hypothyroidism on this medication can live a normal life.

Cancer

Golden Retrievers may be prone to developing several types of cancer, most notably lymphoma, osteosarcoma, and hemangiosarcoma. Lymphoma is cancer of the lymphatic system, and in most cases, begins with tumours in the lymph nodes. In rarer cases, lymphoma can manifest as tumours in other areas, including the skin, gastrointestinal tract, or bone marrow. Lymphoma is typically a disease of ageing, occurring in older Golden Retrievers. Osteosarcoma is bone cancer that most commonly occurs in the leg bones, and also occurs more typically in older Golden Retrievers. Hemangiosarcoma is a cancer of the blood vessels, often characterised by blood-filled tumours.

The cancers that most often afflict Golden Retrievers are frequently aggressive and metastatic, meaning they can quickly spread to other areas, making them difficult to treat. Golden Retrievers with cancer often require pain management and special care related to decreased mobility. In some cases, cancer in Goldens can go into remission with treatment. In other cases, cancers act swiftly and don't respond to treatment.

Your dog will have the best chance of maintaining a prolonged quality of life with early diagnosis. Cancer can cause many different symptoms in dogs, so in general, mention any physical or behavioural changes in your dog that you can't explain. Also, see

Good breeders will do their best to test for genetic problems in their dogs.

Cancer

Cancer can cause many different symptoms, so be sure to mention any physical or behavioural changes to your vet.

your vet if your Golden experiences any of these symptoms:

- Lumps in the lymph nodes, around the neck area
- Masses, lumps, or bumps in any area
- Rashes or any skin or coat changes
- Any indication of bone pain, including limping or yelping when touched
- Weakness or collapse
- Loss of energy, extreme fatigue
- Reluctance to move
- Loss of interest in daily activities
- Pale gums
- Swollen abdomen
- Sudden changes in eating or fluid intake
- Unexplained weight loss or weight gain
- Swelling in any body part
- Appearing depressed, or any change in normal behaviour

In many cases, treatment for cancer in Golden Retrievers is the same as for humans: chemotherapy, radiation therapy, surgery to remove the tumour or afflicted area (often a limb, in the case of osteosarcoma), or a combination of these treatments. Even if your Golden's cancer is incurable, there are many ways you can improve your Golden's remaining time with you by managing pain, increasing comfort, altering diet, and just spending quiet time together. Talk to your vet about the best ways to make your Golden cancer patient more comfortable.

von Willebrand's Disease

This inherited bleeding disorder prevents blood from clotting effectively. Sometimes it is mild, but if a dog undergoes surgery and the vet doesn't know about the disorder, a minor surgery can turn tragic when the dog bleeds to death. While von Willebrand's disease is more common in some breeds than in Goldens, Goldens are occasionally afflicted. The disease is primarily a concern in cases of surgery or injury. A blood test can determine if a dog is afflicted. Ask your breeder if the parents of the puppy you are considering have been tested for von Willebrand's, also called vWD.

Eye Disease

Many breeds are prone to eye diseases. In Golden Retrievers, three eye problems occur most often. Cataracts, sometimes occurring in young dogs, turn the eye lenses opaque, interfering with vision. While cataract surgery is possible and often very effective, it is costly. Retinal dysplasia is a defect of the retina that gradually degrades vision, a particular liability for hunting dogs who depend on their sight. Progressive retinal atrophy is a degenerative retinal disease that eventually results in blindness.

Breeders should have a veterinary ophthalmologist examine their dogs every year, because puppies may have no signs of eye disease, but older dogs may begin to show signs. Responsible breeders will not breed dogs afflicted with heritable eye disease. Ask your puppy's breeder if you can see the results of the eye tests for both the sire and dam, and find out if any Goldens in her breeding programmme have suffered inherited eye conditions.

Know the Signs of Bloat

- Gagging, heavy drooling, inability to vomit
- Pacing, Panting
- Swollen Abdomen

Bloat

Dogs with deep chests are predisposed to developing a serious and often fatal condition called gastric dilation ovules (GDV), otherwise known as bloat. Nobody knows for sure what causes this painful and fast-acting condition, but when it happens, the dog's stomach fills with gas, swells, and twists. This causes the dog severe pain and unless treated immediately with emergency surgery, can result in death. The twisted stomach cuts off blood flow to the stomach, causes a drop in blood pressure, the dog can't burp, vomit, or otherwise get rid of the air and stomach contents, heart function may be compromised, and the dog goes into shock. After one episode of bloat, vets often recommend a special surgery called gastroplexy that attaches the stomach to the abdominal wall to prevent a second occurrence. Dogs that bloat once tend to bloat again, so this surgery is usually a good idea.

Bloat is scary, may or may not be inherited, and seems to favour certain breeds, including Golden Retrievers. Chances are, your Golden won't get bloat. However, many people have theories about ways to reduce the risk, and these are worth practicing. Bloat sometimes occurs right after eating a large meal or drinking a large amount of water, especially right before or right after vigorous exercise, so bloat-prevention strategies mostly involve reducing the chances of this scenario of heavy exercise combined with gulped food:

- Feed your dog more than once a day. Two or even three smaller meals are better than one because if your dog just eats once a

Tick Removal

To remove a tick, first douse it with alcohol. Then, wearing rubber gloves or using a tweezers or special tick remover, pull the tick straight back away from the bite. Don't pull straight up or the head may break off and remain under the skin. Flush the tick immediately, or drop into a cup of alcohol until you can dispose of it.

day, he will probably be so hungry when he eats that he will gulp his food, and air along with it.

- Avoid letting your dog drink large amounts of water while eating. If your dog tends to do this, consider taking away the water dish during dinner, then replacing it about 30 minutes after your dog has eaten. (Just don't forget to put it back!)
- Soak dry food in a little warm water before offering it to your dog. This reduces the amount of air intake while eating.
- If your dog has just been exercising heavily, don't let him gulp water. Let him have a little, then take it away. Offer it again in a few minutes, a little at a time.
- Don't feed your dog right before or after heavy exercise. Wait until he settles down. Immediately call your vet if you witness any signs of bloat. Don't wait! You can't treat bloat at home. Your dog needs treatment for shock and surgery to stabilise the stomach again.

  Signs of bloat include:

- Unsuccessful attempts to vomit, gagging, heavy drooling
- Pacing, panting, unexplained restlessness and agitation
- A swollen, distended abdomen

PEST CONTROL

Fleas, ticks, mosquitoes, worms, mites…these tiny little pests can make life miserable for your Golden Retriever, and a house full of fleas is no picnic for a pet owner, either. These pests do more than irritate your Golden Retriever and make him itch. They can also carry dangerous, even fatal diseases, such as Lyme disease virus. The best way to prevent a pest infestation is through prevention.

Fleas

Fleas multiply quickly and can infest a house almost before you realise they are around. Fleas can carry diseases and their own parasites—like tapeworms—that they can transmit to your Golden Retriever. They can also cause nasty itching, fleabite dermatitis, and allergic reactions. Fleas are, quite simply, tough to kill. That's why they are such good survivors! Fortunately, science has formulated some potent attacks to use against them.

The most effective for most dogs are adulticide spot-ons. The word "adulticide" means the product kills adult fleas. Put a few drops between your Golden Retriever's shoulder blades just once a month.

The product spreads over the skin surface but doesn't enter the bloodstream, making it a safe option for most dogs. A flea that even lands on your dog will die. Some adulticide formulations also kill ticks on contact. Another type of effective product contains an insect growth regulator, or IGR. These keep flea eggs from hatching, so they never grow into adults. These can be topical or come in pill form.

The most popular spot-on adulticides and insect growth regulators are available from your vet, but you can also buy spot-on adulticides and insect growth regulators over the counter in pet stores. Some people say they work just as well as the more expensive prescription brands, and other people insist they are not as effective or safe. Ask your vet for a recommendation.

Other non-prescription flea treatments like flea collars, sprays, powders, and dips, may be cheaper but expose your dog to more pesticides, because they must be used more often to be effective, although for mild infestations, they might work. They also have more side effects.

Finally, non-chemical control works well for the dog who only gets an occasional flea. Regular brushing and a daily once-over with a flea comb during flea season to manually remove fleas may take time, but after the price of the flea comb, it is completely free. Once they are brushed out with the comb, drop fleas into a cup of alcohol to kill them. Giving your Golden Retriever frequent baths also drowns and washes fleas away. Natural botanical shampoos that contain scents that fleas don't like, such as citrus oils and eucalyptus, can also help. These natural methods are popular with pet owners who don't like using flea-control chemicals, or with Goldens who are extremely sensitive to flea control products.

The best way to prevent a flea infestation is through prevention.

Ticks

Ticks can transmit diseases to your Golden Retriever, and also to you. These tiny arachnids swell to many times their normal size when filled with a blood meal. Lyme disease is one of the most common tick-borne

illnesses that can affect both dogs and humans. It is still rare in the UK, but its incidence is increasing. Lyme disease can cause swollen joints and painful arthritis, and serious cases can cause serious heart and kidney damage. If ticks are a problem in your area, consider using an adulticide spot-on that also kills ticks. Also, after time in tick-prone areas, go over your Golden Retriever carefully with a flea comb. If you find a tick, you can remove it manually, but don't use your bare hands. If the swollen tick bursts and you get the blood on your hands, the bacteria can actually infect you through your skin.

Mites

Mites are tiny arachnids that make fleas look large, but they can infest your Golden Retriever's ear canals causing intense itching and irritation. Suspect ear mites if your Golden Retriever scratches frantically and digs at his ears. Another mite is the demodectic mange mite that causes hair loss and may predispose the pet to other skin problems, such as bacterial infections.

Signs of mange mites include intense scratching, scabs, skin flakes like dandruff, and hair loss. See a vet for prescription treatment for mites.

Worms

Many different kinds of worms can infect your Golden Retriever. That is why puppies are routinely wormed, and why, in some countries, dogs should be on heartworm prevention medication to protect against these potentially fatal worms. Roundworms can infect the lungs and intestines, causing a swollen stomach and a poor coat. Hookworms attach to the intestinal wall and can cause anaemia. Whipworms come from ingesting faeces that contain whipworm eggs; they cause diarrhoea, abdominal pain, and weight loss. Tapeworms, usually transmitted by fleas, cause weight loss and diarrhoea.

Roundworms, hookworms, and whipworms are treated with medication available from your veterinary surgeon. The best way to prevent tapeworm is to prevent fleas, but if your dog does get tapeworm, your vet can prescribe medication.

Heartworms are rarely a problem in the UK, but they are fatal if left untreated. They come from mosquitoes, which transmit larvae into the dog's bloodstream. The larvae move into the body, grow into small worms, then move into the heart. Heartworm medication is essential to prevent this dangerous parasite from infecting your Golden Retriever, but your vet will always test for heartworm before giving you a prescription for it. If a heartworm preventive is

Check your Golden for fleas and ticks after he's been outside.

Many people like to add holistic therapies in addition to their dog's conventional health programme.

given to a dog who already has heartworm, it will kill the worms in the heart and they will fatally impede heart function. Treatment isn't always effective, but if your dog gets heartworm, it is your best bet. Preventing mosquito bites is an extra assurance.

HOLISTIC HEALTH

A few decades ago, veterinary surgeons were mostly akin to family practice doctors. They had general training and handled routine care. When a dog developed cancer, hip dysplasia, or heart disease, the answer was usually pretty clear: euthanasia. Today, however, the world of veterinary health care is drastically altered. Specialists and subspecialists use ever-advancing technology to diagnose and treat canine diseases. Veterinary oncologists, cardiologists, ophthalmologists, orthopaedic surgeons, neurosurgeons, and behaviourists with advanced degrees and highly specialised training are common at vet schools, and dogs with diseases that were long considered untreatable have more options than ever before, from chemotherapy and heart surgery to bone transplants and new drug therapies.

That also means vet care is getting pretty expensive, and to some, invasive. As conventional veterinary care continues to advance and evolve, holistic health care for animals is close on its heels, changing and growing in response to an increasing interest in natural healing for humans. This kind of health care is sometimes called holistic, alternative, or complementary, and includes such therapies as acupuncture, homeopathy, herbal medicine, veterinary chiropractic care, pet massage, Reiki, and nutritional therapy. But does holistic health care work?

The Theories Behind Holistic Health Care

Holistic health care is a controversial subject. Some vets vehemently oppose these "alternative" methods. Some find them harmless but not particularly helpful. Some centre their practices around holistic care. It isn't easy to define holistic health care because it means different things to different people and manifests in different ways according to the individual therapy you are talking about. In general, however, the theory behind holistic health care really involves two basic principles: First, holistic health care treats the whole animal (or human), rather than a treatment of a specific disease or set of symptoms in isolation; and second, holistic health care doesn't treat a disease. Instead, it balances and facilitates the body's own ability to heal itself.

For example, if your Golden Retriever is limping, a vet will probably examine the area, do an X-ray, perform some tests including blood work, and ask you to relay a history of symptom development. In a way, this does treat the whole animal—no responsible vet will refuse to look beyond a single afflicted limb. On the other hand, a vet may not ask what you have been feeding your limping animal, where he sleeps, what his home life is like, what other pets are in the house, or other questions seemingly unrelated to the limp. Some vets would find these questions irrelevant. Others do not.

To holistic health care practitioners, every aspect of an animal's life—physical, mental, emotional, spiritual—impacts who that animal is. Bodies flow with blood, oxygen, hormones, and other measurable factors, but also with energy. Bodies also have an amazing capacity for healing themselves when in a balanced state. However, the slightest imbalance to the whole system can upset this complex system, causing a minor disorder that can expand outward. The longer the imbalance remains, the more the whole system goes awry. Outside signs like a skin rash or a limp may be one of the last signs of an internal imbalance that has been going on

Homeopathy

You can find out about homeopathic health care for your Golden by contacting the British Association of Homeopathic Veterinary Surgeons at www.bahvs.com

Holistic care is concerned with the body's balance.

for weeks, months, even years.

Anything can cause system imbalance: a traumatic experience, a physical injury, a poor diet. The flow of energy through the body's meridians becomes disrupted, so that somewhere in the body, energy builds up or is blocked, like a river with a dam. In holistic health, a limp is not just a limp. It is a signal of imbalanced energy that you can't see on an X-ray or measure by a blood test. Until that imbalance is corrected, the symptom can only be masked, not resolved. For this reason, holistic health doesn't typically endorse treatments that mask symptoms. Instead, it treats the source of the symptom, correcting the balance, so the body can heal itself.

This means that holistic health care does not provide cures, or even treatments, for diseases and conditions. This is a common misconception about holistic health care, and a reason why the term "alternative medicine" is misleading. This form of health care is not medicine, per se, but it does treat a problem: the body's basic imbalance. It puts the body in ideal condition for self-healing. When energy blockages are freed, the body can unleash its own healing power. That is why holistic therapies take much longer than conventional therapies to show any sign of working. The body is healing itself, gradually, in stages. But, proponents say, the final effect is more profound.

This whole business sounds pretty strange to a lot of people, and holistic health care is certainly not for everyone. However, for those who adhere to holistic therapies for themselves, this ancient attitude towards healing makes a lot of sense. On the other hand, anyone using holistic therapies must—for the sake of their pets—understand the limitations of this kind of health care. First of all, conventional medicine is best for acute conditions and aggressive diseases: trauma, broken bones, heart failure, aggressive cancer, respiratory distress, heat stroke, etc. Holistic therapies can add to the treatments for these conditions but cannot match conventional care, with its continuing innovations and technology, in speed and effectiveness. Chronic conditions like allergies and arthritis, as well as general anxiety-related conditions like nervousness, shyness, and separation anxiety, on the other hand, can benefit from holistic therapies, especially when practitioners use the best of both worlds, as appropriate: the technologies and innovations of conventional medicines as necessary, coupled with the gentle healing boost natural therapies may provide. For instance, a glucosamine supplement and periodic pet massage can decrease pain and increase mobility in an arthritic Golden Retriever, but if mobility is completely lost or pain is unmanageable, stronger pain-relieving drugs and/or hip surgery may be a more appropriate treatment.

In other words, conventional and complementary therapies can work best together, either at the same time or one followed by the eventual need for the other, as appropriate. Holistic therapies can't set a broken bone, repair a faulty heart valve, or remove a cancerous tumour, but they might be able to help the body better cope with allergies, shore up the immune system in a dog being treated for cancer, or help calm an anxious Golden Retriever.

If you decide to seek out holistic care for your Golden Retriever, please do so in consultation with your regular vet. Some herbal remedies can work against certain prescription medications. Not every diet works well for every dog. Physical therapy coupled with chiropractic manipulation may be redundant at best, or in the worst case, work against each other. Also, seek your holistic health care practitioners carefully. Look for those who also have veterinary degrees and who have advanced training and a good reputation. Ask for recommendations and do your research. If everyone on your Golden's health care team communicates, your Golden Retriever has the best chance at glowing good health.

Chronic Conditions

Chronic conditions like allergies and arthritis can benefit from holistic therapies.

Popular Holistic Health Therapies

Many different therapies fall under the umbrella of holistic health, from acupuncture to flower remedies to pet massage. Some of these have studies behind them supporting their positive effects on the body. Others are primarily supported mostly by anecdotal evidence. Each has its supporters and detractors. Here is a brief description of some of the more popular holistic health therapies.

Acupuncture

The practitioner inserts thin, flexible needles at certain key points in the body to release the flow of energy. Most dogs tolerate this very well and don't seem to be bothered by needle insertion. Benefits may include pain relief in arthritic dogs and improved immune response. Some studies and anecdotal evidence support acupuncture's positive effect on pain and mobility.

Flower Remedies

These gentle remedies contain the essence of flowers, but not the actual flowers. Flowers are steeped in purified water, then removed. Different flowers are thought to address different emotional conditions on an energetic level, and many people believe they can help with anxiety, shyness, nervousness, fear, or hyperactivity. The flower remedy is typically added to the dog's water. Most evidence for the effectiveness of flower remedies is anecdotal.

Herbal Medicine

The practitioner prescribes herbal remedies to treat various conditions, often based on ancient knowledge about which herbs treat which conditions. Many animal supplement companies are now doing additional research to study the efficacy of various herbal remedies. A few herbal supplements are becoming widely accepted as beneficial. Glucosamine and chondroitin sulfate have been shown to have a positive effect on joint pain and mobility in arthritic animals. Others, like pennyroyal oil or comfrey, have been shown to be dangerous for animals. Some herbal remedies can react negatively with conventional medications, so always tell your vet if your Golden is taking an herbal remedy.

Homeopathy

The practitioner administers medicines containing ingredients that would cause the very conditions they are meant to relieve. The theory is that if a substance causes a symptom in a healthy animal (or person), a highly diluted form of the same substance will cure those same symptoms in someone already experiencing them. While many people endorse this form of treatment, no clear-cut studies have demonstrated any positive effects from homeopathic remedies.

A combination of traditional and holistic therapies might be right for your dog.

Nutritional Therapy

This nutritional approach to health care operates on the sensible principle that what you eat affects your health. Typically, nutritional therapy advocates home-cooked, sometimes raw, diets for dogs and doesn't support processed dry food. Providing your dog with adequate nutrition via a home-prepared diet is difficult, however, so be sure you have information from a good source.

Pet Massage

Similar to massage in humans, pet massage can help to increase mobility and relieve pain in joints afflicted with arthritis. Many dogs love to be massaged, others don't care for it. Find an experienced, certified pet massage therapist. Many massage therapists have turned over their practice to pets because of the increasing popularity of this therapy, which actually physically increases circulation in muscles and soft tissues while gently manipulating joints to improve range of motion.

Reiki

The practitioner manipulates an animal's (or human's) energy, often without even touching the animal, and even via long distance. This therapy is controversial, not because it can do any harm but because some people don't see how it can possibly have any effect. Others swear by it. The practitioner should have extensive training and should be able to explain to you how Reiki works.

FIRST AID: WHAT TO DO IN AN EMERGENCY

If you are lucky, you may never have to deal with an emergency situation with your Golden Retriever. However, it could happen, and in an emergency situation, seconds count. If your dog is injured or suffers an acute episode, knowing what to do and being prepared can make a big difference on your Golden's prognosis. Before an emergency, the prepared pet owner will already have the following:

- Emergency first-aid kit
- Phone number and address of your vet, who will have arrangements in place for 24-hour cover
- An on-call family member or friend to help you, if necessary
- Blankets and/or towels (these can stop bleeding, stand in as tourniquets, or serve as a stretcher)
- A strip of cloth or gauze to use as a muzzle, just in case
- Training in CPR and the Heimlich manoeuvre for pets

If you find yourself in an emergency situation, try to remain calm, for the sake of your dog. Get the situation under control, then phone the vet or emergency clinic. Here are some of the more common veterinary emergencies, and what to do if they happen to your Golden.

Car Accident

If your Golden Retriever gets hit by a car, he could be seriously injured internally, even if you don't see any marks on him. If your dog can walk, take him to a veterinary surgery. If he cannot walk, first get him and yourself out of the way of traffic, then take him to a vet. Move an immobilised dog very carefully, preferably with

Emergency Kit

Every pet owner should have an emergency first-aid kit, just in case. Keep it in an easily accessible location at home, and take it with you when you travel with your Golden. Your emergency kit should contain:

- Phone number and address of your veterinary surgeon
- A copy of your dog's medical records
- A picture and identifying information about your dog
- Your own name, address, and phone number, in case you lose the kit
- Gauze pads
- Rolled gauze or cotton bandages
- Bandage tape
- Scissors for cutting bandages and tape
- Hydrogen peroxide
- Hydrocortisone ointment or cream
- Antibiotic ointment or cream
- Eye wash
- Tweezers
- Oral syringe
- Benadryl and dosage information from your vet, for your individual dog
- Heavy blanket for warmth or to use as a stretcher
- Towel to help stop bleeding
- Thermometer
- Bottled water

the help of another person by lifting him onto a towel or blanket and moving the blanket. Moving an injured dog could make his injuries worse. Remember to protect yourself, too. An injured dog can bite out of pain and fear—yes, even your dog. If your dog shows signs of extreme pain, wrap a strip of cloth gently around his muzzle to keep him from biting.

If your dog is bleeding, try to stop the bleeding before you take him to the vet, or on the way while someone else drives you. Apply pressure with a towel or bandage to the wound until the bleeding stops and the wound begins to clot. This could take awhile, depending on the severity of the injury. If bleeding won't stop, keep applying pressure until you can get your dog help. When the bleeding stops or slows, bandage the wound securely until you can get to the vet. In extreme cases where you can't get veterinary help right away, tie a piece of cloth above the wound, not so tight that you cut off all circulation but tight enough to help slow bleeding. (This only works on appendages.)

Keep an eye on your Golden puppy for his health and safety.

Even if your dog looks perfectly fine, take him to the vet anyway, just in case. The chances of internal injury are too great to risk your animal's health.

Animal Fight

If your Golden Retriever gets in a fight with another dog, you may need to treat bleeding wounds. Rinse wounds with an antiseptic solution like hydrogen peroxide and apply pressure to stop bleeding. When bleeding stops or slows, bandage the wound securely until you can get to the vet. If the fight was a severe one with a much stronger animal, seek veterinary care immediately, even if your Golden seems to be fine. As with a car accident, your Golden could have internal injuries that won't reveal themselves until later, when they will be much more difficult to treat. Injuries

In the case of an emergency, remember to stay calm, for the sake of your Golden.

from other animals can also contain bacteria and your vet may want to give your Golden antibiotics to safeguard against infection.

Choking

Goldens love to chew, and puppies love to try to chew anything they can get their mouths around. If your Golden Retriever puppy or adult begins to cough and paw at his mouth, appearing extremely distressed and not breathing, he is probably choking on a hard object and you must act quickly. You can injure your Golden if you try to do the following techniques and he isn't really choking, so be as sure as possible. Then, try the following:

1. First open his mouth and swoop through with your hooked finger to dislodge the object, being careful not to push it further in. If you can't see anything, don't probe your Golden's throat.
2. If you can't dislodge the object, hold your Golden's hind legs and lift him up (if you can), which could dislodge the article.
3. If this doesn't work, hit your Golden between the shoulder blades sharply with your palm, which could bring up the object.
4. If this doesn't work, stand behind your Golden Retriever, wrap your arms around him, make a fist with one hand and place it under your Golden's ribcage, then cover it with your other palm. Now, using a quick sharp motion, press in and up to dislodge the article, in the style of the Heimlich manoeuvre.
5. If this doesn't work after just a few tries, get to the vet immediately.
6. If you are able to dislodge the object, take your Golden to the vet for a follow-up check, to be sure he hasn't suffered internal injury.

CPR

If your Golden Retriever's heart stops beating and/or he stops breathing for any reason—drowning, trauma, heart attack—you can try CPR in order to help keep your dog alive until he can receive veterinary care. Check for signs of breathing and heartbeat before attempting CPR to avoid injuring your dog. Signs of breathing include chest rising and falling and condensation on a small mirror held in front of your dog's nose. If your dog's heart is beating, you should be able to feel it by placing your hand on the left side of your dog's chest.

Ideally, someone can drive you and your dog to the vet or emergency clinic while you perform CPR. Some classes offer instruction on these techniques for pets, or your vet may be willing to demonstrate. Even without training, however, you might be able to save your Golden Retriever. Here's how:

1. First, make sure your Golden's airway is unobstructed. Open his mouth and look inside. If you see anything blocking the airway, hook it out with your finger, being careful not to push it farther in. If necessary, follow instructions above for choking.
2. If or when the airway is clear and your Golden still isn't breathing, begin artificial respiration with your Golden lying on his side.
3. Put your Golden's head in a position so that his neck is straight. Hold his muzzle closed with your hand and put your mouth over his nose.
4. Exhale quickly and forcefully into his nose four times; repeat, giving about 20 breaths per minute.
5. Feel for a heartbeat. If you can't feel one, begin chest compressions by placing your knee behind your Golden, and your palm on your Golden's ribcage at the spot where his elbow would press against his chest. Put your other hand on top.
6. Press sharply five times in a row, about twice per second.
7. Give your Golden another breath through his nose.
8. Repeat compressions at the rate of about five compressions in three seconds per breath, until you reach help.

Finally, in the case of an emergency, remember to stay calm, for the sake of your Golden. Dogs have an inborn instinct to look to humans for guidance, and quickly pick up on our emotional state. If you exude calm reassurance, your Golden Retriever may feel calmer and be less likely to injure himself further. No matter how

CPR

If you have a chance and your vet is willing, ask him or her to demonstrate CPR and how to dislodge an object from your Golden's throat. If you've seen them performed before you ever need to use it, you'll be much more confident in an emergency.

Once your Golden Retriever reaches the age of six or seven, it is time to be vigilant about the annual veterinary checkup.

upset you are, remember that your Golden takes his cues from you.

THE AGEING GOLDEN

We all hope our Goldens will live long, healthy lives, but Goldens age just like we do, and unfortunately, their lifespan doesn't match ours. Many Golden Retrievers live to be 9 or 10. A few lucky ones reach 12 or even 15 years. But that means that most dog owners will eventually have to deal with the ageing and death of their beloved pets.

As Golden Retrievers age, they require more frequent veterinary visits and attention to physical and behavioural changes. Veterans are not only more prone to the diseases of ageing like heart disease and cancer, but to decreased energy and mobility, and the deterioration of other organs, including the brain. Dogs can experience dementia similar to Alzheimer's disease, called Canine Cognitive Dysfunction. They can have decreased vision, decreased hearing, decreased kidney function. Just as when your Golden is young, keep an eye out for any changes in behaviour and habits, to catch these conditions early.

Many symptoms people normally associate with ageing are actually signs of treatable disease, and your Golden Retriever doesn't have to suffer.

Veteran Care

Some veteran dogs—like some older people—simply don't act their age. They run, play, retrieve, and don't require any change in diet or care, right up until their final days. In most cases, however, older dogs (like older people) start to slow down a bit as they age. When a dog's activity level goes down, so should his calorie intake, to prevent him from becoming overweight. An inactive dog simply doesn't need to eat as much. That doesn't mean you need to switch to a so-called senior / veteran diet, but limiting treats and slightly decreasing portion size is appropriate.

Once your Golden Retriever reaches the age of six or seven, it is time to be vigilant about the annual veterinary check-up. Your vet may want to add some extra tests to your Golden's regular check-up regimen, and this is a good idea. Many diseases to which Goldens are prone are diseases of ageing, and many are treatable. Regular check-ups and tests can catch these diseases early, significantly increasing the chances of treatment success. Also, be even more careful about noticing and recording any changes in your Golden Retriever's skin, coat, movement, diet, and behaviour. Keep up with that grooming journal and you'll have a good written record. Finally, when your older dog does start to slow down, consider how you can make him more comfortable:

- For dogs with limited vision, don't move furniture around. Keep things in their familiar places.
- For dogs with decreased hearing, don't sneak up on them or touch them when they are sleeping.
- Be patient with slow movement and the occasional wish to be left alone. Sometimes older dogs just get cranky and sore and don't want attention.

A good diet and lots of exercise can keep your senior Golden healthy.

- Be patient with dogs who seem to need extra attention and reassurance. As your dog nears the end of his life, you will want to remember that you spent a lot of time together.
- Consider foam padding for your dog's bed. This can prevent bedsores in bedridden dogs and make sore joints more comfortable. Cover the foam with a soft blanket.
- For arthritic dogs, consider a heated bed or heated insert for your dog's bed.
- For dogs with rear leg lameness, as with advanced hip dysplasia, look into a rear leg harness/lead. These leads slip over the back legs and hold them up, so the dog doesn't have to put so much weight on the hip joints but can still feel like he is walking more easily. This can also help a lame dog with relieving himself.

Be your dog's advocate. Ask questions of the vet, learn about any conditions he has, and do whatever you can to minimise suffering.

Saying Goodbye

When your Golden does reach the stage where he no longer enjoys quality of life and has pain that can't be managed, you may have to consider whether it is time to euthanise him. This is one

Finding a Lost Dog

Your Golden is lost! Losing your precious pet can be terrifying, but time is of the essence. Your chances of recovering your dog are much higher if he is wearing identification tags and/or has an identifying microchip. It is also good to have a clear, identifying photo of your pet to show people in case he gets lost. Identification tags are by far the most effective way to recover a wandering pet, but you can further maximise your chances of recovering your lost pet by being proactive:

- Look all over the area and ask people if they have seen your dog. Bring a picture.
- Physically visit the rescue centre nearest to you daily to see if your dog has been brought in. Don't just call, actually go there. Also, phone or post signs at rescue centres in surrounding areas.
- Post as many signs as you can in the area, even beyond where you think your dog might wander. Post on public bulletin boards in high-traffic locations, areas near where you lost your dog, and at veterinary surgery, rescue centres, dog parks, and pet stores. Posters are more effective with pictures.
- Place a classified ad describing your dog and offering a reward. Leave out one identifying feature so you can be sure people who call you actually have your dog.
- Beware of people who will try to get you to pay them money first or meet you in a secluded location—they may not even have your dog, and this is a common scam. Meet strangers with a buddy in a public place. If someone actually has your dog, they will probably be happy to describe your dog in great detail and to return him to you without any reward. (Of course, a reward is nice to give a truly honest person who went out of the way to help you get your dog back.)

of the toughest decisions pet owners ever have to make. People who go through this and have a close relationship with their pet often say that they knew when their pet was ready to go. This varies immensely between pets, and their people. Some can't seem to tolerate suffering, while others seem to want to hold on for a while. Just remember to base your actions on what is best for your Golden, not yourself. Your veterinary surgeon can help you to make this difficult decision.

Living with an ageing Golden isn't always easy. Expensive treatments, low energy, behavioural changes, loss of bladder and bowel control, confusion, and lack of mobility can all make the pet owner's life more difficult. But remember how much your Golden has given you throughout his lifetime. Our dogs love us and devote their lives to us. When they age or become ill, you have the opportunity to give back just a fraction of the love your Golden has given you. Getting the chance to be loved by a Golden Retriever is a rare and wonderful thing.

But losing a Golden Retriever is difficult and can involve serious prolonged grief. Give yourself time to recover. Let yourself reflect back on the good times. Seek help, in the form of the many resources for pet loss in bookstores and on the Internet. Talk to a counsellor if you feel unable to get past your grief, and know that you are not alone.

Finally, remember how very lucky you are that a Golden Retriever has changed your life. A dog loved you, and that means something. Your Golden Retriever was lucky to have you, too.

APPENDIX

KENNEL CLUB BREED STANDARD

General Appearance: Symmetrical, balanced, active, powerful, level mover; sound with kindly expression.

Characteristics: Biddable, intelligent and possessing natural working ability.

Temperament: Kindly, friendly and confident.

Head and Skull: Balanced and well chiselled, skull broad without coarseness; well set on neck, muzzle powerful, wide and deep. Length of foreface approximately equals length from well defined stop to occiput. Nose preferably black.

Eyes: Dark brown, set well apart, dark rims.

Ears: Moderate size, set on approximate level with eyes.

Mouth: Jaws strong, with a perfect, regular and complete scissor bite, i.e. upper teeth closely overlapping lower teeth and set square to the jaws.

Neck: Good length, clean and muscular.

Forequarters: Forelegs straight with good bone, shoulders well laid back, long in blade with upper arm of equal length placing legs well under body. Elbows close fitting.

Body: Balanced, short-coupled, deep through heart. Ribs deep, well sprung. Level topline.

Hindquarters: Loin and legs strong and muscular, good second thighs, well bent stifles. Hocks well let down, straight when viewed from rear, neither turning in nor out. Cow-hocks highly undesirable.

Feet: Round and cat-like.

Tail: Set on and carried level with back, reaching to hocks, without curl at tip.

Gait/Movement: Powerful with good drive. Straight and true in front and rear. Stride long and free with no sign of hackney action in front.

Coat: Flat or wavy with good feathering, dense water-resisting undercoat.

Colour: Any shade of gold or cream, neither red nor mahogany. A few white hairs on chest only, permissible.

Size: Height at withers: dogs: 56-61 cms (22-24 ins); bitches: 51-56 cms (20-22 ins).

Faults: Any departure from the foregoing points should be considered a fault and the seriousness with which the fault should be regarded should be in exact proportion to its degree and its effect upon the health and welfare of the dog.

Note: Male animals should have two apparently normal testicles fully descended into the scrotum.

March 1994

AMERICAN KENNEL CLUB BREED STANDARD

General Appearance: A symmetrical, powerful, active dog, sound and well put together, not clumsy nor long in the leg, displaying a kindly expression and possessing a personality that is eager, alert and self-confident. Primarily a hunting dog, he should be shown in hard working condition. Overall appearance, balance, gait and purpose to be given more emphasis than any of his component parts. Faults—Any departure from the described ideal shall be considered faulty to the degree to which it interferes with the breed's purpose or is contrary to breed character.

Size, Proportion, Substance: Males 23-24 inches in height at withers; females 21?-22? inches. Dogs up to one inch above or below standard size should be proportionately penalized. Deviation in height of more than one inch from the standard shall disqualify. Length from breastbone to point of buttocks slightly greater than height at withers in ratio of 12:11. Weight for dogs 65-75 pounds; bitches 55-65 pounds.

Head: Broad in skull, slightly arched laterally and longitudinally without prominence of frontal bones (forehead) or occipital bones. Stop well defined but not abrupt. Foreface deep and wide, nearly as long as skull. Muzzle straight in profile, blending smooth and strongly into skull; when viewed in profile or from above, slightly deeper and wider at stop than at tip. No heaviness in flews. Removal of whiskers is permitted but not preferred. Eyes friendly and intelligent in expression, medium large with dark, close-fitting rims, set well apart and reasonably deep in sockets. Color preferably dark brown; medium brown acceptable. Slant eyes and narrow, triangular eyes detract from correct expression and are to be faulted. No white or haw visible when looking straight ahead. Dogs showing evidence of functional abnormality of eyelids or eyelashes (such as, but not limited to, trichiasis, entropion, ectropion, or distichiasis) are to be excused from the ring. Ears rather short with front edge attached well behind and just above the eye and falling close to cheek. When pulled forward, tip of ear should just cover the eye. Low, hound-like ear set to be faulted. Nose black or brownish black, though fading to a lighter shade in cold weather not serious. Pink nose or one seriously lacking in pigmentation to be faulted. Teeth scissors bite, in which the outer side of the lower incisors touches the inner side of the upper incisors. Undershot or overshot bite is a disqualification. Misalignment of teeth (irregular placement of incisors) or a level bite (incisors meet each other edge to edge) is undesirable, but not to be confused with undershot or overshot. Full dentition. Obvious gaps are serious faults.

Neck, Topline, Body: Neck medium long, merging gradually into well laid back shoulders, giving sturdy, muscular appearance. No throatiness. Backline strong and level from withers to slightly sloping croup, whether standing or moving. Sloping backline, roach or sway back, flat or steep croup to be faulted. Body well balanced, short coupled, deep through the chest. Chest between forelegs at least as wide as a man's closed hand including thumb, with well developed forechest. Brisket extends to elbow. Ribs long and well sprung but not barrel shaped, extending well towards hindquarters. Loin short, muscular, wide and deep, with very little tuck-up. Slab-sidedness, narrow chest, lack of depth in brisket, excessive tuck-up to be faulted. Tail well set on, thick and muscular at the base, following the natural line of the croup. Tail bones extend to, but not below, the point of hock. Carried with merry action, level or with some moderate upward curve; never curled over back nor between legs.

Forequarters: Muscular, well coordinated with hindquarters and capable of free movement. Shoulder blades long and well laid back with upper tips fairly close together at withers. Upper arms appear about the same length as the blades, setting the elbows back beneath the upper tip of the blades, close to the ribs without looseness. Legs, viewed from the front, straight with good bone, but not to the point of coarseness. Pasterns short and strong, sloping slightly with no suggestion of weakness. Dewclaws on forelegs may be removed, but are normally left on. Feet medium size, round, compact, and well knuckled, with thick pads. Excess hair may be trimmed to show natural size and contour. Splayed or hare feet to be faulted.

Hindquarters: Broad and strongly muscled. Profile of croup slopes slightly; the pelvic bone slopes at a slightly greater angle (approximately 30 degrees from horizontal). In a natural stance, the femur joins the pelvis at approximately a 90-degree angle; stifles well bent; hocks well let down with short, strong rear pasterns. Feet as in front. Legs straight when viewed from rear. Cow-hocks, spread hocks, and sickle hocks to be faulted.

Coat: Dense and water-repellent with good undercoat. Outer coat firm and resilient, neither coarse nor silky, lying close to body; may be straight or wavy. Untrimmed natural ruff; moderate feathering on back of forelegs and on underbody; heavier feathering on front of neck, back of thighs and underside of tail. Coat on head, paws, and front of legs is short and even. Excessive length, open coats, and limp, soft coats are very undesirable. Feet may be trimmed and stray hairs neatened, but the natural appearance of coat or outline should not be altered by cutting or clipping.

Color: Rich, lustrous golden of various shades. Feathering may be lighter than rest of coat. With the exception of graying or whitening of face or body due to age, any white marking, other than a few white hairs on the chest, should be penalized according to its extent. Allowable light shadings are not to be confused with white markings. Predominant body color which is either extremely pale or extremely dark is undesirable. Some latitude should be given to the light puppy whose coloring shows promise of deepening with maturity. Any noticeable area of black or other off-color hair is a serious fault.

Gait: When trotting, gait is free, smooth, powerful and well coordinated, showing good reach. Viewed from any position, legs turn neither in nor out, nor do feet cross or interfere with each other. As speed increases, feet tend to converge toward center line of balance. It is recommended that dogs be shown on a loose lead to reflect true gait.

Temperament: Friendly, reliable, and trustworthy. Quarrelsomeness or hostility towards other dogs or people in normal situations, or an unwarranted show of timidity or nervousness, is not in keeping with Golden Retriever character. Such actions should be penalized according to their significance.

Disqualifications: Deviation in height of more than one inch from standard either way. Undershot or overshot bite.

Approved October 13, 1981
Reformatted August 18, 1990

ORGANISATIONS

Breed Clubs and Kennel Clubs

American Kennel Club (AKC)
5580 Centerview Drive,
Raleigh, NC 27606
Telephone: 919 233 9767
Fax: 919 233 3627
E-mail: info@akc.org
www.akc.org

Canadian Kennel Club (CKC)
89 Skyway Avenue, Suite 100
Etobicoke, Ontario M9W 6R4
Telephone: 416 675 5511
Fax: 416 675 6506
E-mail: information@ckc.ca
www.ckc.ca

Federation Cynologique Internationale (FCI)
Secretariat General de la FCI
Place Albert 1er, 13B – 6530
Thuin, Belqique
www.fci.be

Golden Retriever Club
General Enqiries Clive Donahue
E-mail: clive-donahue@supanet.com
http://www.thegoldenretrieverclub.co.uk

Golden Retriever Club of America (GRCA)
P.O. Box 69
Berthoud, CO 80513
www.grca.org

Golden Retriever Club of Scotland
Membership Secretary Miss Lesley Wilson
8a Heath Avenue, Lenzie,
Glasgow,G66 4L6
Telephone: 01417 762312

Golden Retriever Club of Wales
Secretary Mrs Frankie Prosser
Glannant, Nantddu,
Cwmtaff, Merthyr Tydfil,
CF48 2HY.
Tel: 01685 371761
www.grcw.org.uk/

The Kennel Club
1 Clarges Street
London, W1J 8AB
Telephone: 0870 606 6750
Fax: 0207 518 1058
www.the-kennel-club.org.uk

United Kennel Club (UKC)
100 E. Kilgore Road
Kalamazoo, MI 49002-5584
Telephone: 269 343 9020
Fax: 269 343 7037
E-mail: pbickell@ukcdogs.com
www.ukcdogs.com

Pet Sitters

National Association of Registered Petsitters
www.dogsit.com

UK Petsitters
Telephone: 01902 41789
www.ukpetsitter.com

Dog Services UK
www.dogservices.co.uk

Rescue Organisations and Welfare Groups

British Veterinary Association Animal Welfare Foundation (BVA AWF)
7 Mansfield Street
London W1G 9NQ
Telephone: 0207 636 6541
Fax: 0207 436 2970
Email: bva-awf@bva.co.uk
www.bva-awf.org.uk/about

Golden Retriever Club of Scotland Rescue
Mr & Mrs E Fogg
Telephone: 01738 624751

Golden Retriever Club of Wales Rescue
Mrs C Miles, Pontypool,
Telephone: 01495 772960

Golden Retriever Rescue
Mrs L Blankenspoor
Telephone: 01242 238068
Mrs G Robinson
Telephone: 01580 752210

Royal Society for the Prevention of Cruelty to Animals (RSPCA)
Telephone: 0870 3335 999
Fax: 0870 7530 284
www.rspca.org.uk

Scottish Society for the Prevention of Cruelty to Animals (SSPCA)
Braehead Mains, 603
Queensferry Road
Edinburgh EH4 6EA
Telephone: 0131 339 0222
Fax: 0131 339 4777
Email: enquiries@scottishspca.org
www.scottishspca.org/about

Sports

Agility Club UK
www.agilityclub.co.uk

British Flyball Association
PO Box 109, Petersfield
GU32 1XZ
Telephone: 01753 620110
Fax: 01726 861079
Email: bfa@flyball.org.uk
www.flyball.org.uk

International Agility Link (IAL)
Global Administrator Steve Drinkwater
E-mail: yunde@powerup.au
www.agilityclick.com/

World Canine Freestyle Organisation
P.O. Box 350122Brooklyn, NY 11235-2525
Telephone: (718) 332-8336
www.worldcannefreestyle.org

Therapy

Pets As Therapy
3 Grange Farm Cottages
Wycombe Road, Saunderton
Princes Risborough
Bucks HP27 9NS
Telephone: 0870 977 0003
Fax: 0870 706 2562
www.petsastherapy.org

Therapy Dogs International (TDI)
88 Bartley Road
Flanders, NJ 07836
Telephone: (973) 252-9800
Fax: (973) 252-7171
E-mail: tdi@gti.net
www.tdi-dog.org

Training and Behaviour

Association of Pet Dog Trainers (APDT)
PO Box 17
Kempsford GL7 4W7
Telephone: 01285 810811

Association of Pet Behaviour Counsellors
PO Box 46
Worcester WR8 9YS
Telephone: 01386 751151
Fax: 01386 750743
Email: info@apbc.org.uk
www.apbc.org.uk

British Institute of Professional Dog Trainers
http://www.bipdt.net

Veterinary and Health Resources

Association of British Veterinary Acupuncturists (ABVA)
66A Easthorpe, Southwell
Nottinghamshire NG25 0HZ
Email: jonnyboyvet@hotmail.com
www.abva.co.uk

Association of Chartered Physiotherapists Specialising in Animal Therapy (ACPAT)
52 Littleham Road
Exmoouth, Devon EX8 2QJ
Telephone/Fax: 01395 270648
Email: bexsharples@hotmail.com
www.acpat.org.uk

British Association of Homoeopathic Veterinary Surgeons
Alternative Veterinary Medicine Centre
Chinham House
Stanford in the Vale
Oxfordshire SN7 8NQ
Email: enquiries@bahvs.com
www.bahvs.com

British Association of Veterinary Opthalmologists (BAVO)
Email: hjf@vetspecialists.co.uk
Email: secretary@bravo.org.uk
www.bravo.oprg.uk

British Small Animal Veterinary Association (BSAVA)
Woodrow House,
1 Telford Way
Waterwells Business Park
Quedgley, Gloucester
GL2 2AB
Telephone: 01452 726700
Fax: 01452 726701
Email: customerservices@bsava.com
www.bsava.com

British Veterinary Association (BVA)
7 Mansfield Street,
LondonW1G 9NQ
Telephone: 020 7636 6541
Fax: 020 7436 2970
E-mail: bvahq@bva.co.uk
www.bva.co.uk

British Veterinary Hospitals Association (BHVA)
Station Bungalow
Main Road, Stockfield
Northumberland NE43 7HJ
Telephone: 07966 901619
Fax: 07813 915954
Email: office@bvha.org.uk
www.BVHA.org.uk

Royal College of Veterinary Surgeons (RCVS)
Belgravia House, 62-64
Horseferry Road, London
SW1P 2AF
Telephone: 0207 222 2001
Fax: 0207 222 2004
Email: admin@rcvs.org.uk
www.rcvs.org.uk

Newspapers and Magazines

Dog World Ltd
Somerfield House
Wotton Road, Ashford
Kent TN23 6LW
Telephone: 01233 621877
Fax: 01233 645669

Dogs Today
Town Mill, Bagshot Road
Chobham, Surrey GU24 8BZ
Telephone: 01276 858880
Fax: 01276 858860
Email: enquiries@dogstodaymagazine.co.uk
www.dogstodaymagazine.co.uk

Kennel Gazette
Kennel Club
1 Clarges Street
London W1J 8AB
Telephone: 0870 606 6750
Fax: 0207 518 1058
www.the-kennel-club.co.uk

K9 Magazine
21 High Street
Warsop
Nottinghamshire NG20 0AA
Telephone: 0870 011 4114
Fax: 0870 706 4564
Email: mail@k9magazine.com
www.k9magazine.com

Our Dogs
Our Dogs Publishing
5 Oxford Road
Station Approach
Manchester M60 1SX
www.ourdogs.co.uk

Your Dog
Roebuck House
33 Broad Street
Stamford
Lincolnshire PE9 1RB
Telephone: 01780 766199
Fax: 01780 766416

Books

Barnes, Julia
Living With a Rescued Dog
Dorking: Interpet Publishing, 2004

Evans, J M & White, Kay
Doglopaedia
Dorking: Ringpress, 1998

Evans, J M
Book of The Bitch
Dorking: Ringpress, 1998

Tennant, Colin
Mini Encyclopedia of Dog Training & Behaviour
Dorking: Interpet Publishing, 2005

Evans, J M
What If my Dog?
Dorking: Interpet Publishing, 2005

Websites

Responsible Dog Breeding
www.britishdogbreeders.co.uk
A cornucopia of information and pertinent links on responsible dog breeding for British breeders.

Dog Behaviour
www.dogbehaviour.com
Canine Behaviourist Gwen Bailey's site, filled with useful advice on canine behaviour, communication, and relevant links.

Petfinder
http://www.pet-locator.co.uk/
Search shelters and rescue groups for adoptable pets.

The Golden Retriever Club
www.thegoldenretrieverclub.co.uk
This site covers every topic related working Golden Retrievers from conformations to field trials, and offers an extensive list of rescue organisations throughout England, Scotland, Ireland, and Wales.

Reading

Barrie, Anmarie. *Dogs and the Law*. Neptune City: T.F.H. Publications, Inc., 1990.

Gerritson, Resi, and Rudd Haak. *K9 Schutzhund Training: A Manual for Tracking, Obedience, and Training*. Alberta: Detselig Enterprise, 2000.

Middleton, Joseph. *Top Dog: Training the Retriever for Waterfowl and Upland Hunting.* New York: Dutton Books, 2004.

Rubenstein, Eliza, and Shari Kalina. *The Adoption Option: Choosing and Raising the Shelter Dog for You.* New York: Howell Books, 1996.

Serpell, James. *The Domestic Dog: Its Evolution, Behaviour and Interactions with People.* Cambridge: Cambridge University Press, 1995.

Spencer, James. *Training Retrievers for the Marshes and Meadows*. Loveland: Alpine Publications, 1998.

INDEX

ACKNOWLEDGMENTS

Thanks to the many people and organisations who contributed their vast knowledge to this book, especially the Golden Retriever Club of America, the American Kennel Club, and the many Golden Retriever breeders, judges, handlers, and owners I have spoken to over the years. Thanks also to Fritz, the Golden Retriever who walks his people by our house every day, for his jolly ways and exuberant lust for life. He may be a little bit big, a little bit red, and a little bit wild, but he has the great big golden heart of his brethren.

ABOUT THE AUTHOR

Eve Adamson is an award-winning pet writer and the author of over 30 books, including *The Guide to Owning a Bulldog, The Simple Guide to Grooming Your Dog, Your Outta Control Adopted Dog,* and *The Simple Guide to a Healthy Dog,* which won the 2003 Eukanuba Canine Health Award for the best published work devoted to improving the health of dogs. She is a contributing editor for Dog Fancy magazine and writes monthly for many other pet-related publications, such as the *AKC Gazette, Your Dog* (the Tufts Veterinary School Newsletter), *Dogs USA, Puppies USA,* and the *Popular Dogs* series. She also writes a grooming column for AKC *Family Dog* magazine, as well as both the breed profile and "Natural Dog News" columns for *Pet Product News* magazine. She lives in Iowa City with her partner, two children, two adopted dogs, a parakeet, and a hamster.

PHOTO CREDITS

Jan Stadlemyer (Shutterstock): 14, 186
Josiah J. Garber (Shutterstock): 130
Ritika Dewan (Shutterstock): 137
Tim Elliot (Shutterstock): 195
All other photos courtesy of Isabelle Francais.